MARTHA'S VINEYARD TALES

FROM PIRATES ON LAKE TASHMOO TO BAXTER'S SALOON

CHRIS BAER

Globe
Pequot

Guilford, Connecticut

Globe Pequot

An imprint of The Rowman & Littlefield Publishing Group, Inc.
4501 Forbes Blvd., Ste. 200
Lanham, MD 20706
www.rowman.com

Distributed by NATIONAL BOOK NETWORK

British Library Cataloguing in Publication Information available

Library of Congress Cataloging-in-Publication Data

Names: Baer, Chris, author.
Title: Martha's Vineyard tales : from pirates on Lake Tashmoo to Baxter's Saloon / Chris Baer.
Description: Guilford, Connecticut : Globe Pequot, [2017]
Identifiers: LCCN 2018001170 | ISBN 9781493034697 (hardcover)
Subjects: LCSH: Martha's Vineyard (Mass.)—History, Local. | Martha's Vineyard (Mass.)—Social life and customs. | Martha's Vineyard (Mass.)—Biography.
Classification: LCC F72.M5 B | DDC 974.4/94—dc23 LC record available at https://lccn.loc.gov/2018001170

∞™ The paper used in this publication meets the minimum requirements of American National Standard for Information Sciences—Permanence of Paper for Printed Library Materials, ANSI/NISO Z39.48-1992

Printed in the United States of America

In memory of Stan Lair (1902–1987)

ACKNOWLEDGMENTS

To my wife, Janice, and my son, Jack, for their unwavering support. To my mom and dad, Jackie and Gene Baer, for their story ideas, memories, and encouragement.

To Jamie Stringfellow and Geoff Currier at the *Martha's Vineyard Times* for their commas, apostrophes, and confidence.

And to all the wonderful people who chimed in on Facebook posts, answered my emails, took my calls, and helped solve a lot of curious mysteries.

CONTENTS

INTRODUCTION

When you imagine nineteenth-century Martha's Vineyard, whaleships and widow's walks might come to mind, or perhaps fishermen and farmhands. Androids may not. And yet in 1883, a set of androids was patented by Edgartown inventor Richard Shute. Titled "Androides or Automaton Shoe-Factory," Shute's invention consisted of eight miniature robotic shoemakers with moving arms and bodies, who labored over little shoes at their benches, buffing tiny soles and swinging miniature hammers when the spring was wound.

Small, curious stories like this one fill these pages. Some are bizarre, some are quirky, some are sad, some are touching, some are familiar, some are just awful, and many are surprising. All are true. And all are quite human. I hope this book will challenge some common views of Martha's Vineyard history and poke holes in a few of the old stereotypes.

This is not a textbook. It is intended to be opened anywhere and enjoyed; it's a book more for the nighttable than the classroom. It's intended to be whimsical, not stuffy. Nevertheless, I take the research for these stories very seriously.

This is not meant to be a comprehensive history of the Island, by any means. There are loads of important events that I've skipped over entirely; most have been well covered elsewhere. But I hope this book will hold a few surprises even for those who feel they are pretty familiar with Vineyard history.

The majority of these stories were adapted from my column in the *Martha's Vineyard Times*, "This Was Then," and were published in some form between 2014 and 2017. But there are lots of unpublished bits here as well that I hope you will enjoy.

My grandfather's photographs were the germ for the majority of these stories. More often than not, I began with an old photo, and then tried to find the story behind it. I fell down more than a few Symmes Holes along the way. I have some favorites: "The Joggins," "Tivoli Girl," "The Artist Mystic," "The Cottage City Carnival of 1882," and "Welcome and the Ape" among them, mostly because they were completely unfamiliar to me. Many were particularly fun to write, like "Journey to the Center of the Earth" and "Old Island Cooking." Others were based on larger-than-life Island characters whom I have doggedly chased for years, like George Cleveland ("Arvagasugiaqpalauqtut Kinguvaanginnik Qaujinasungniq"), Edson Chick, George Fred, and Rodolphus Crocker and his boys ("Shugrue" and "The Wooden Leg").

There are no morals to these stories, except, perhaps, that humans and their behaviors have not changed much.

Enjoy.

PART I
EARLY ISLAND TALES

MARTIN'S VINEYARD

U m, what's the island called, again? Actually, historians have never been able to agree on what the original English name was, nor its namesake. To start with, was it "Martha's" or "Martin's"?

In 1602, English explorer Capt. Bartholomew Gosnold came ashore on what is now called Nomans Land. In his published account, chronicler John Brereton wrote:

> At length we were come amongst many faire Islands . . . but comming to an anker under one of them, which was about three or foure leagues from the maine, captaine Gosnold, my selfe, and some others, went ashore, & going round about it, we found it to be foure English miles in compasse, without house or inhabitant, saving a little old house made of boughes, covered with barke, an olde piece of a weare of the Indians, to catch fish, and one or two places, where they had made fires.

In the margin, Brereton added, "The first Island called Marthaes vineyard." (In a later account he added, "The rest [of the Island was] overgrowne with trees, which so well as the bushes, were so overgrowne with Vines, we could scarce pass them." So although grapes are mentioned nowhere in any of Gosnold's accounts, perhaps "Vineyard" still has a relatively clear provenance.)

Detail from "A Map of New England and New York" [John Speed, 1676]

Gosnold was not the first European to visit our Island. Italian explorer Sebastian Cabot sailed past nearly a century earlier, as did Giovanni da Verrazzano shortly afterward; both made rough maps of the coastline, and for all we know may have even landed here. Verrazzano named an island southwest of Cape Cod "Luisa," which has been tentatively attributed to modern Block Island, but some historians speculate that "Luisa," named after the mother of the king of France, could have been the Vineyard.

When Gosnold first landed in New England (somewhere north of Cape Cod, possibly Cape Ann) in 1602, he was greeted by a group of native men in a "Basque-shallop with mast and sail." Their native leader wore shoes and stockings, waistcoat, breeches, hat and band, with his eyebrows painted white, and spoke and understood some English. Sailing south around the Cape to our islands and ultimately camping for about a month on "Elizabeth's Isle" (likely modern Cuttyhunk), Gosnold's men had several more encounters with English-speaking natives. "They pronounce our language with great facility," writes Brereton, "for one of them one day sitting by me, upon occasion I spake smiling to him these words: How now (sirrah) are you so saucy with my tobacco? . . . [He] spoke so plain and distinctly, as if he had been a long scholar in the language."

There were two chroniclers aboard—Gabriel Archer being the second—and both wrote popular accounts of Gosnold's voyage, which later inspired other English explorers to seek adventures in America. Their accounts are similar. They describe the island-hopping Wampanoag inhabitants as confident, well organized, eager to trade, and happy to assist the Englishmen in cutting sassafras, worth a small fortune in England. They "offered themselves unto us in great familiarity," wrote Archer.

The Wampanoags were tall—"of stature much higher than we"—and wore their hair long, tied up in a knot and adorned with feathers, they wrote, and drank from large cups "made like skulls." They wore deerskin loincloths, "much like a blacksmith's apron" and "make beards of the hair of beasts: and one of them offered a beard of their making to one of our sailors, for his that grew on his face, which because it was of a red color, they judged to be none of his own." They offered local furs for trade, including beaver, luzerne, martin, otter, wild-cat, black fox, and seal skin. Only one ugly incident marred their visit: Toward the end of their month or so of island living, a couple of Gosnold's men had a fight with one of their native chaperones, and one Englishman received a minor arrow wound.

Gosnold's chroniclers described the islands as covered with "high-timbered oak," cedar, beech, elm, holly, walnut, and cherry, together with a wide variety of berries, and a freshwater lake full of small tortoises. "In every island, and almost in every part of every island, are great store of ground-nuts, forty together on a string, some of them as big as hen's eggs; they grow not two inches under ground; the which nuts we found to be as good as potatoes," Brereton wrote.

Gosnold's original plan to leave a group of planters behind to start a colony or trading post was soured by the lack of supplies, and by concerns about the Wampanoags following the arrow incident. "Some of our company that before vowed to stay [began] to make revolt," wrote Archer. They returned to England with a fortune in sassafras and some new names which stuck: "Cape Cod," "Elizabeth Island(s)," and "Marthaes"—or was it "Martin's"?—Vineyard.

Was "Martha's" or "Martin's" the name Gosnold intended? Historian Charles Banks in his classic book *History of Martha's Vineyard* points out that in some 85 percent of seventeenth-century written references to our Island, it's spelled "Martin's Vineyard" rather than "Martha's Vineyard." (The name was also quickly transferred from Nomans to its larger neighbor to the north.) Even Thomas Mayhew Sr., who acquired the title to the Island and established the first English settlement here, called it Martin's Vineyard. The first book of Island deeds is titled "Upon Martin's or Martha's Vineyard," although most seventeenth-century legal documents dodged the issue by abbreviating it "Mart. Vineyard." "The name 'Martin's' was used up to about 1700," writes Banks, "even by the residents of the Vineyard, by local historians and cartographers, by public officials throughout New England and New York."

But who could "Martin" have been? It's believed that Gosnold was accompanied on this voyage by a Capt. John Martin, better known for his later associations with Gosnold in Jamestown Colony. Gosnold named other minor locales after his traveling companions (like "Point Gilbert" for Bartholomew Gilbert, and "Tucker's Terror" after another fellow traveler), so it would be no surprise if he named the Vineyard after his shipmate Captain Martin, who was after all the son of the former lord mayor of London.

It wasn't until the eighteenth century—after Gosnold and Brereton were long dead—that "Martha's" became the more popular choice for the name. And there are some solid theories as to who "Martha" could have been. Gosnold had an infant daughter named Martha who had died (probably a few years before his voyage); however, historians are skeptical that an explorer of that era would name an island after a deceased child. A better candidate is Gosnold's influential mother-in-law, Martha Golding, who helped find the financial backing for his 1602 voyage. But then why a full century of "Martin's Vineyard" first?

Captain Martin is best known as one of the founding settlers and original leaders of Virginia Colony at Jamestown in 1607, together with Gosnold. He was scrappy, ambitious, and a survivor, but he was not well liked. He was seen as privileged, combative, and a complainer. He was quarrelsome, uncooperative, "embroiled in controversies," and even refused to pay taxes. The planters complained about him to the London Company, writing, "Captain Martin hath refused to submitt himselfe to the lawes."

So was it the dead baby, the contentious captain, or the rich mother-in-law? We could have worse name options. Three years after Gosnold's visit, French explorer Samuel de Champlain spotted the Island and named it "La Soupçonneuse" ("The Suspicious One") because "in the distance we had several times thought it was not an island." The name entered French culture as "l'Ile Douteuse" (Doubtful Island).

Maybe Gosnold should have asked the inhabitants of that little old house made of boughs. The Wampanoag "Noëpe" might have been the best choice after all.

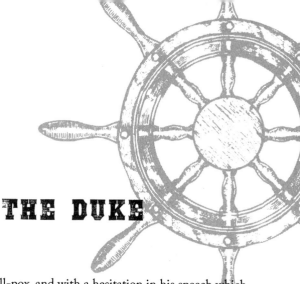

THE DUKE

"Pitted with small-pox, and with a hesitation in his speech which at moments of excitement made him difficult to understand, there was nothing in the appearance of the Prince to touch a young maid's fancy," wrote author Martin Haile in a biography of the duke's second wife, Mary of Modena.

Meet the duke of Dukes County.

James, Duke of York, was the second son of King Charles I of England. In 1663 he purchased Martha's Vineyard, Nantucket, Maine, and Long Island from the Earl of Stirling for a total of thirty-five hundred pounds. (He ultimately failed to pay a penny of it, but kept legal possession anyway.) The next year, the king gifted him New Netherland as well, and then sent four warships to take it from the Dutch. The newly seized province was renamed "New York" in the duke's honor, and the Vineyard officially became part of provincial New York.

In 1683 New York established its first twelve counties, including four royally named ones: Queens (now a "borough"), Kings (better known today as "Brooklyn"), Dutchess (named for Mary of Modena, Duchess of York), and Dukes (which at this time included Nantucket). Alas, the duke himself never set foot on the Vineyard.

James ascended the British throne in 1685 upon the death of his older brother, and became known as King James II. His suspected

The duke of Dukes County

Catholicism made him an unpopular monarch, however; he was deposed just three years later in the Glorious Revolution and fled to France, remaining in exile for the remainder of his days.

Dukes County did not become a part of Massachusetts until 1691.

1743: Esther, a Native American slave being delivered from Boston to her North Carolina master on the sloop *Endeavor*, broke her restraints, stole a longboat, and escaped, while stopped overnight in Edgartown harbor. "How she got loose we know not," reported the *New York Morning Courier*.

THE COURTHOUSE

The Dukes County Courthouse, built in 1858 from local brick, is by no means the first courthouse on the Vineyard. The first trial on record on Martha's Vineyard was likely held in the home of Governor Mayhew in 1677–78, when a fine was imposed for an "unseemly Act in the governers house." A much more serious trial took place in 1689, when a Wampanoag man named Pammatoock was charged for "killing Sarah an Indian maid at tisbury" more than two decades earlier. He was found guilty and ordered to be "executed . . . until he is dead dead dead."

The Dukes County Courthouse, Edgartown

It was the first known execution on the Island, and probably took place in Edgartown.

Our first dedicated courthouse was built in 1721, but the choice of Edgartown as the county seat was immediately challenged. Chilmark lawyer Major Pain(e) Mayhew—who is often referred to, perhaps fittingly, as "Major Pain"—was the first to attempt to force the move of our county seat to Chilmark or Tisbury. He failed, but the battle had only begun. In 1764 a second courthouse was built in Tisbury, and for more than forty years the county maintained not one, but two Island courthouses.

1768: During a violent February hailstorm in Chilmark, lightning struck the house of Jonathan Tilton, went down his chimney, and instantly killed the twenty-five-year-old man and the dog lying beside him. Five others in the house were also struck down and injured. [*Hartford Courant*]

DR. GELSTON'S SMALLPOX HOSPITAL

The Vineyard's first public hospital was an experimental and highly controversial institution dedicated to smallpox inoculation.

Smallpox visited the Island with tragic regularity during the colonial era, and none worse than the epidemic of 1763–64. A catastrophic disease decimated the Wampanoags that same winter, which many historians believe was also smallpox. Thirty-nine Vineyard Wampanoags died, mostly on Chappaquiddick, as did two-thirds of the Native American population of Nantucket (some 222) sealing the fate of their long-term survival as a people on that island.

The Town of Tisbury responded to the unfolding tragedy in 1763 by granting arriving physician Dr. Samuel Gelston "Liberty to Carry on Inoculation of the Small Pox at Homses Hole" provided that he would take local smallpox victims into his care, and that he would pay the town six shillings for every non-resident he inoculated. It was among the very first such inoculation hospitals opened in colonial America. The exact location of Dr. Gelston's hospital is forgotten, but his contract with the town was renewed again the next year. Dr. Gelston practiced an experimental and quite controversial procedure known as "variolation"—the inoculation of a healthy patient with a (hopefully) weak strain of live smallpox virus in a controlled setting. The death rate from

Seth Daggett, a housewright and carpenter who settled near Tashmoo spring, served on the committee to oversee Dr. Samuel Gelston's short-lived and experimental smallpox hospital at Holmes Hole in 1764. Daggett died of smallpox in 1779 and was buried near his home at the Overlook where he and his wife Elizabeth had raised their nine children.

variolation was a sobering 2 to 3 percent, but it provided long-term immunity to a scourge which would ordinarily kill 20 to 30 percent of its victims.

In 1771 Dr. Gelston constructed a new hospital on Gravelly Island, a now-vanished islet between Muskeget and Tuckernuck off the west coast of Nantucket, but at that time technically a part of Edgartown.

Residents of Nantucket, unnerved by this new institution and fearful of an accidental outbreak, petitioned the Commonwealth to annex Gravelly Island to Nantucket in order to stop Dr. Gelston's experiments. The colonial authorities responded by prohibiting all inoculations on Gravelly Island, and in 1778 Nantucket authorities purchased Dr. Gelston's buildings for the tidy sum of one thousand pounds, and unhesitatingly razed them. (Another century passed before Muskeget and Gravelly Island were formally taken from Edgartown and given to Nantucket; Gravelly Island has since been lost to erosion.)

Undeterred, Dr. Gelston erected his next inoculation hospital at Cape Poge. It only lasted a few months before Edgartown authorities changed their minds; it may have been responsible for the 1778–79 outbreak that killed Rev. Samuel Kingsbury of Edgartown's Congregational Church as well as Tashmoo farmer Seth Daggett, who ironically had been on the town committee charged with monitoring the doctor's original experiments in Holmes Hole.

1787: Isaac Coombs, thirty-nine, of Gay Head, was executed in Salem for the murder of his wife, Sage. A fifer during the Revolution who later joined a tribe of Mohawks near Montreal, Coombs beat his wife to death while "much in drink." He gave a full confession to his jail keeper.

WARNED OUT

One of the main functions of town government in the 1700s and 1800s on Martha's Vineyard, or anywhere in the Commonwealth, was caring for those in need. The selectmen of the Town of Tisbury, for instance, also carried the second title of "Overseers of the Poor" until it was split off as its own elected position just before the Civil War. Funds for the poor were the single biggest line item in Tisbury's annual budget—typically two or three times the funds allocated for schools or highways, for instance.

After John Rogers of Tisbury died in 1780, a meeting was called "to See what Method the Town will take to provide for two of John Rogeses Children that is now on the Towns Cost at the Rate of two Silver Dollars per week. Either to Vandue them off at the Lowest bidder or to provide for them Some other way . . ." (The word *vendue* is an old-fashioned term for a public auction.)

When new families arrived and fell on hard times, the bill for their care was sent to their legal town of residence. Selectmen were regularly entangled in lawsuits in which the residence of a destitute family was in question, as the Rogers family's was with the town of Middleborough. By 1794, the length of time required to establish residency in any Massachusetts town was lengthened to a full ten years (except for the rich and the well connected).

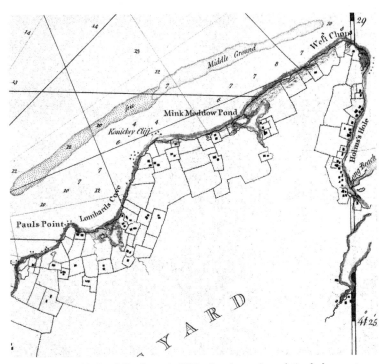

Tisbury, as charted by Joseph Des Barres in 1781, when the town's population had grown to a little over one thousand residents. Now get out.

Towns sometimes acted to remove new arrivals before they became legal residents—either because they were at risk of becoming a liability to the town, or for other unwanted traits. They were said to be "warned out."

In 1790 the constable of Tisbury warned Abigail Allen, widow, and Sarah Allen, spinstress, to "Depart the Limmits of the Town of Tisbury within fifteen Days." In 1791, Abisha Pease Jr. and his family were warned "to depart out of the town of Tisbury," as was mariner Elijah Daggett, his wife Peggy, and their kids. (The Daggetts evidently soon returned; in 1799 the town voted to pay the doctor's bill for Elijah's final illness and for the support of his widow Peggy and their seven young children.)

Immigrants who fell into need but had no "settlement" (legal residence) were considered "state paupers" rather than "town paupers." By the mid-1800s, this usually meant being taken to an off-Island poorhouse or the state orphanage. The "Laws of Settlement" were complex. Slaves were originally given the settlement of their master, but after slavery was abolished in Massachusetts in 1780, the children of former slaves sometimes found themselves without any legal residence at all, and were left to the responsibility of the state. Native Americans, considered wards of the state, also usually found themselves "unsettled."

In 1883, Eunice Rocker, an impoverished woman of both Native and African-American descent, lived in her Cottage City home with her eight children. Her husband Antone, a Chilean seaman and fish peddler, had died two years earlier. Although her family had lived on the Island for generations (if not millennia), Rocker and her family were declared "unsettled," and Cottage City's Overseers of the Poor issued warrants for their removal to the Tewksbury Almshouse. Two constables were sent to their home to transport them, but the Rockers held their ground with "irons, hot water, and hot fat," according to the *Boston Globe*, and as the violence escalated, with a hammer and an axe as well. Both constables were seriously injured, and several members of the Rocker family were charged with assault. The authorities finally succeeded in removing the family to Tewksbury, but they were soon discharged and were able to return to their Vineyard home.

1801: A line of telegraphs was completed, extending from Holmes Hole to the outskirts of Boston. News was relayed visually, using semaphore telegraph machines sighted by telescopes and operating along a string of carefully positioned "telegraph hills." The arrival of the ship *Mercury* from Sumatra to the Vineyard in 1801 was among the first news items successfully relayed. Boston merchants paid handsomely for timely news from Holmes Hole, one of the busiest ports on the Atlantic coast.

THE MAILMAN AND
THE SHOEMAKER'S BOY

Forty-three-year-old mail carrier Ansel Dimmick of Falmouth set off one cold January evening in 1816 with mail bound for Holmes Hole. "The sound was much obstructed with ice," reported the *New York Evening Post*, "and the passage very difficult and dangerous, and impracticable by small boats." With him was James Freeman, sheriff of Barnstable County, and Falmouth hatter Amaziah Wilcox. They never made it. Wilcox's body, the boat, and the mail were found five days later on West Chop, and Freeman's body was found the next day at Eastville. Dimmick's body was never found. "All have left widows & large families of children indigent," wrote the minister who attended their funerals.

Rev. Charles B. Ray, who spent his early years in a Holmes Hole shoemaker's shop. He became a leading national abolitionist and publisher of the Colored American.

The view from the Vineyard Haven Methodist Church steeple before the Great Fire of 1883, looking down Church Street, with Union Wharf (built 1835) in the background. The large house with the smoking chimneys in the right foreground, built about 1790, was owned by Oliver Crosby during the early 1800s; Robinson's shoemaking shop would have been on the far right-hand side of Crosby's property, on the corner of what is now known as Union Street.

But the mail must go through. Appointed in Dimmick's place in this dangerous job was Joseph Ray, a thirty-seven-year-old African-American sailor from Rhode Island, likely born a slave. Ray was by now a professional mariner, holding a Seamen's Protection Certificate he had been issued a decade earlier. He carried the mail to and from the Vineyard in his open sailboat for the next thirty years, bringing the mail in the worst of weather from Falmouth to Holmes Hole and on to Edgartown. His wife is said to have been an escaped slave who had once been harbored by abolitionist families in Falmouth. Traveling lecturer Samuel Gould wrote of leaving the Vineyard in 1837, "From Martha's Vineyard

I crossed over to Falmouth, with Mr. Ray, an estimable colored citizen of Falmouth. Mr. Ray . . . has the reputation of being the best navigator in the Sound."

Not long after he began his job in 1816, Ray placed his son Charles into an apprenticeship with shoemaker Thomas Robinson of Holmes Hole, to labor in his shoemaking shop on the northeast corner of Main Street and what is now called Union Street, formerly known as Wharf Street.

Although later in life Charles was remembered fondly by his white peers from the Vineyard, their memories focused mostly on the leather strap Robinson used to beat him. In 1832 Ray left the Island to become the first black student to enroll at Wesleyan University; however, his time there lasted less than two months, as white students immediately demanded his removal. Charles Bennett Ray would become a leading abolitionist and one of the most distinguished black leaders of his day. He published what was by 1840 the most important African-American newspaper in the United States, the *Colored American*, and as an active "conductor" of the Underground Railroad, Ray was personally involved in helping southern families escape slavery. His daughter Charlotte eventually became the first African-American woman to pass the bar and become a practicing lawyer in the United States.

In 1827, Captain Coleman of the sloop *Levant* sighted a creature off Gay Head which, according to the report he gave to the *Nantucket Inquirer*, "he adjudges to be the far famed sea-serpent. The creature had a head shaped some-what like that of a horse with nostrils through which he appeared to breathe. The head and neck were about 6 or 8 feet out of the water; and the circumference of the body at the surface seemed about that of a barrel. It progressed in the water with an undulatory motion . . . and the whole length seemed about 60 feet."

While Coleman's serpent seems ridiculous today, at least one Island sailor had already been lost to a monstrous reptile: In 1802, news reached Edgartown that thirty-year-old native son Tristram Cleveland "fell overboard and was eaten by an Alligator in the Harbour of Batavia" leaving his wife and a four-year-old daughter to mourn his loss. Batavia was located in Java, East India—today known as Jakarta, Indonesia, where the offending creature was probably a crocodile rather than an alligator. Cleveland's widow died in Edgartown eighteen years later at the age of fifty-two. "She had passed thro a Sea of Trouble," recorded the Rev. Joseph Thaxter in her burial record.

CRINKLE, CRINKLE, CRANGLE

In 1851, the *Vineyard Gazette* reported that twenty-eight-year-old Merinda Smith was standing by the open window of a cooper's shop on Main Street in Vineyard Haven, singing, when she was struck by lightning and "received a charge of electricity in the mouth, which paralyzed her tongue, and rendered her speechless." She survived, and eventually recovered her voice. (Her husband Gustavus avoided a mortal fate of another kind twelve years later, when he was narrowly acquitted for the island's only axe-murder, still unsolved.)

But nature evidently wasn't content with merely paralyzing young singers that week. Tragedy struck only two days later when a second horrendous lightning storm descended on Vineyard Haven. The storm killed two villagers and injured another three or four in other parts of the island. Vineyard Haven painter Francis Nye Jr. was struck and instantly killed while working in the basement of his paint shop where the store bank stands today, as was Mrs. Elwina Norris, widow of the infamous captain of the *Sharon* mutiny, while relaxing with friends in her home.

The *Gazette* wrote of Mrs. Norris's tragic end: "The lightning descended through the roof, and shattered the whole house considerably. The fluid came out over the mantle piece in the room in which

Mrs. Norris was sitting, with several friends, and is supposed to have entered her ear. It slightly scorched her neck, but there was no other trace of it on her person. She was instantly killed. No other person was injured to any extent. The hands on the clock were melted, as also the brasses which supported the fire set. . . . The cloud from which the electric fluid was discharged, hung directly over Holmes Hole for twenty or thirty minutes, during which time there was an almost uninterrupted flash of lightning and roar of thunder. The scene was frightful and appalling, and made the stoutest hearts to quail."

• • •

Stories of an unusual epitaph have made the rounds since at least 1861. Some accounts say it is on a stone in Chatham, others described it as a tablet next to a cedar pole near the Holmes Hole lighthouse. The story has it that two or three friends (or in some tellings, brothers) were out in a small sloop (or, alternately, taking shelter under a cedar tree) when the men (either from Holmes Hole, or heading for it) were killed by a bolt of lightning. Many variations of the epitaph have been reported, but most go something like this:

> *There were three brothers went to sea*
> *Who were never known to wrangle*
> *Holmes' Hole,*
> *Cedar Pole,*
> *Crinkle, crinkle, crangle.*

Some reports describe zigzag lines engraved next to the epitaph, which together with the last line, were intended to suggest an electrifying event.

• • •

The *New York Sun* reported in 1876, "A widow at Martha's Vineyard is exhibiting the house in which her husband was killed by lightning. Admission costs twenty-five cents, and the curiosities to be seen are a shattered bedstead, broken mirrors, and a photograph of the man after death."

"An Old Sailor," corresponding with the *Boston Globe* in 1894, recalled visiting Holmes Hole in the 1840s: "I have a pleasant recollection of the place as a great emporium for mutton pies, excellent mittens and stockings and as the home of a kind-hearted people."

BURIED TREASURE

In gale winds and heavy seas in the fall of 1850, the bark *Missouri* of New York, loaded with a cargo of Indonesian pepper and twenty-five thousand dollars in silver dollars, was wrecked on the northwest coast of the island of Sumatra. Samuel N. Dixey, twenty-three, of Marblehead was in command, having taken over the voyage after the death of the original captain.

"Before it could be got out," reported the *New York Daily Tribune*, "the natives began to fire muskets from the beach at the crew who fled to the boats alongside, leaving Captain Dixey upon deck alone. At night the natives came off, robbed the vessel of the money, tied Capt. D.'s hands and feet together and fastened him by the neck to a gun. Ship *Sterling* was in the immediate vicinity, and the crew of the *Missouri* proceeded to her. Capt. Pitman of the S., with both crews, went to the wreck next day and released Capt. D."

Only this was a lie. When the *Sterling* arrived at the scene of the wreck, its twenty-nine-year-old captain, Henry Pitman, proposed an idea to Captain Dixey of the *Missouri*: Steal the coins and concoct a story about a theft. Dixey agreed, and they secretly transferred kegs full of Mexican pillar dollars (popularly known as "pieces of eight") into sacks, hid them aboard the *Sterling*, and smuggled their treasure back to the United States the following winter. Captain Dixey spent his share on a lavish European tour. Captain Pitman chose to play it safe, and to instead bury eight thousand dollars on the beaches of a laid-back little harbor known as Holmes Hole (renamed Vineyard Haven in 1871).

So Pitman and his second mate went ashore at what is now Vineyard Haven Harbor, "on the point, in a creek near the boathouse," and buried thirteen bags of silver coins. Pitman measured the distance to the boathouse with his feet, and made a mental treasure map: ten feet east and twenty-four feet south of the boathouse. Time passed.

In February 1852, Captain Pitman sent his brother William to the Vineyard to fetch his silver. William befriended twenty-five-year-old Clifford Dunham of Holmes Hole and paid him four hundred dollars to help him locate and retrieve the coins, and then to sail him to Falmouth in an open boat at two o'clock in the morning. Dunham borrowed a neighbor's boat and made the crossing in the dark, but grounded before they could reach the beach. Pitman was forced to wade through the frigid, waist-deep February waters to reach the shore of what is now Falmouth Heights. Freezing, he sloppily reburied the silver in the dark upon Great Hill Beach, removed his wet boots, and ran barefoot two miles to the train station in Falmouth. Dunham sailed home and slept through the next day, exhausted. When he awoke, Dunham told his story to Thomas Bradley, the local justice in Holmes Hole, and surrendered his four-hundred-dollar payment.

William Pitman was arrested that afternoon at the New Bedford railroad depot by US marshals, his hands and feet badly frostbitten, carrying a carpetbag containing sixteen pounds of silver dollars. Soon both Pitman brothers and Captain Dixey were all under arrest. The charges against William were dropped on a technicality (he had been charged with "plunder" when the crime was declared to be "embezzlement"), but Capt. Henry Pitman and Captain Dixey were both found guilty. Dixey was sentenced to five years in Dedham Jail, Pitman to three years in Salem Jail. In 1854, two years into Pitman's sentence, however, and for reasons that remain unclear, US president Franklin Pierce took an interest in Pitman's case and granted him a full presidential pardon. He went on to have a long and prestigious maritime career in California. Clifford Dunham of Holmes Hole went on to become a captain of his own ship—the bark *Scotland*, of Boston—but died in Havana of yellow fever in 1854 at the age of twenty-eight. His gravestone can be found in West Chop Cemetery.

1855: The Rev. Charles Brooks presented a paper at a meeting of the Association for the Advancement of Science in Providence, titled "Remarks on Intermarriage of Blood Relations," which caused an uproar when word reached the Island. Brooks declared, "At Martha's Vineyard they have a particularly bad time. The island is a sea-girt. The youths cannot go a courting elsewhere, because of the rolling billows, and so they content themselves with Marthas in the Vineyard.... [Consequently,] their minds are moderate; their health is feeble." [*Albany Evening Journal*]

TWO FUGITIVE TALES

In 1854, Edinbur Randall, a stowaway fugitive slave from Alabama, stole a boat and escaped from the lumber bark *Franklin* while anchored in Holmes Hole, northbound from Florida. Acting upon advice he had been given by sympathetic sailors on the *Franklin*, Randall found refuge with the Wampanoag in Gay Head. When deputy sheriff Thomas Lambert arrived with a warrant for his arrest on a charge of stealing the boat, Randall hid in a swamp. Beulah Vanderhoop of Gay Head then disguised him in a woman's dress and bonnet and brought him to the home of her grandmother, Mrs. Peters, who threatened to scald the sheriff with a kettle of hot water if he tried to cross her threshold. Hiring a pair of local sailors to take him to New Bedford in the dead of night, Randall found safety in the home of a New Bedford abolitionist.

Four years later, in 1858, a similar situation played out a little differently: A fugitive slave named Philip Smith (possibly a pseudonym) was discovered concealed in a steward's pantry on board the northbound brig *William Purrington* of Wilmington, North Carolina. Upon arriving at Holmes Hole, the captain, fiercely determined to return the slave, purchased a pair of irons to restrain him and threatened to shoot the first person attempting to come aboard to try to rescue him. When the deputy sheriff arrived with a posse of policemen to serve papers to the captain, it was discovered that the fugitive had escaped—evidently by swimming to shore through frigid December waters upon a plank. It was believed Smith reached Boston on a sloop, and eventually escaped to Canada.

1860: Captain Otis Tilton of Edgartown, master of the ship *John* of New Bedford, and his crew were reportedly "taken by natives" on the South Pacific and killed in 1852. But in 1860, rumors reached Edgartown that Tilton was not dead but rather engaged in the slave trade and that Tilton had been seen, bearing an assumed name, and identified by some of his former crewmen. The rumor was of particular interest to his widow and children on the Vineyard.

THE SEMINARY

In 1868, the Rev. Horace Barrows Marshall moved to the Vineyard from Maine with his wife Annie and their three young sons. A graduate of what is now Colby College, Reverend Marshall came to serve as the new pastor of the Holmes Hole Baptist Church, a tall white wooden church that dominated the center of town until the Great Fire of 1883 burned it to the ground.

In the summer of 1870, Reverend Marshall erected a substantial new building, the Grove Hill Seminary, on a hill north of Holmes Hole, across from what is today the Unitarian Church on Main Street. It was a private school (possibly girls-only for a time). Marshall soon quit his job as pastor to become its principal.

The seminary was not particularly successful. Marshall moonlighted as the acting pastor of the West Tisbury Baptist Church, and after the birth of their fourth son Philip in 1873, the Marshalls closed the school and moved to Chelmsford.

Mrs. Love West, who for many years had been the proprietress of the Mansion House, bought the vacant seminary building and renovated it as a hotel, which she named the Grove Hill House. It became a popular and successful summer hotel for more than twenty years, and was a favorite gathering spot each summer for Army and Navy officers and their families from Washington, DC. When the Great Fire burned down all of downtown Vineyard Haven, including the Mansion House,

Grove Hill became a refuge for many local families made homeless by the inferno.

One of those Army officers was evidently Lieut. Col. Charles Barnett, an elite West Point graduate who served as deputy quartermaster general of the US Army. His status in Washington was such that his elaborate Baltimore wedding to Miss Sallie Shoemaker was attended by Gen. William Sherman (of Civil War fame) and the sitting president himself, Rutherford Hayes.

The Barnetts purchased the hotel upon Mrs. West's retirement, renamed it Avenel, and converted it to a summer home. Along with their two sons, Charlie Jr. and Eccleston, the Barnetts summered at Avenel until 1902, when Colonel Barnett was sent to a sanatorium in Battle Creek, Michigan, for "suicidal mania," and jumped to his death from its fourth floor at the age of fifty-seven.

Colonel Barnett's son Charlie, a civil engineer, lived at Avenel for another quarter-century. A concrete expert, he designed a number of Vineyard Haven's concrete buildings, including Renear's Showroom on Church Street (today known as Church Street Landing) and Vineyard Haven's concrete water standpipe. Alas, in 1936 he followed his father's dark path and intentionally shut himself in Avenel's garage with a running automobile, ending his life at the age of fifty-one. Avenel—the former seminary—was demolished not long afterward.

The names of the students who attended Grove Hill Seminary have been forgotten, except for two: Ellis Manter and Harriet Eaton, who attended the school as teenagers. Both grew up with modest means. (Harriet's mother died when she was less than two weeks old, and she grew up on her grandparents' farm.) Both came into wealth in their lifetimes, and both bequeathed significant sums to the community. The Harriet (Eaton) Goldberg fund is now part of the Permanent Endowment for Martha's Vineyard, and the Ellis Manter fund, managed by the Tisbury School, continues to provide shoes, clothes, and other necessities for students in need.

JOURNEY TO THE CENTER OF THE EARTH

The word "Chops"—as in East and West—derives its name from the business end of a mouth, the parts one might lick, or (proverbially, anyway) bust. While still a geographically rare name, there is another famous example: The English Channel also has chops.

Between our chops is the harbor known in the nineteenth century as "Holmes Hole," or, earlier, "Homes Hole." Like nearby "Woods Hole," "Quick's Hole," and "Robinson's Hole," the name refers to an opening, a mouth. As Charles Banks wrote in *The History of Martha's Vineyard*, "It is probably derived from 'Homes,' meaning an old man, and the entire name signifies 'old man's hole.' . . . The word 'homes' indicates decrepitude as applied to an aged person, and probably was applied to an old chief who made this place his abode when the first settlers, in 1642, came to the island."

Holmes Hole was renamed "Vineyard Haven" in the early 1870s—residents were tired of living in a "hole"—but the name lived on in some unusual circles.

In 1818, Army officer John Symmes of St. Louis published his theory—actually a variation on some very old legends—that "the earth is hollow, and habitable within," with vast openings at both the North and South Poles. Inside was a "warm and rich land, stocked with thrifty vegetables and animals if not men." His theory was widely circulated, and equally widely discredited, but never fully squashed. The alleged openings became known as "Symmes Holes," and his theories would inspire much science fiction, most notably Jules Verne's popular 1864 novel, *Journey to the Center of the Earth.*

Edward Everett, who had served as both US secretary of state and governor of Massachusetts, decried in a well-publicized 1861 speech, "The Causes and Conduct of the Civil War," "There is, I am aware, no end to human credulity. Captain Symmes and his numerous followers were persuaded that the earth is as hollow as a gourd and that you can sail into the interior as easily as a Down-East coaster can sail into Holmes' Hole."

As often happens, the stories became garbled, and soon after Everett's speech, Symmes's hypothetical hole at the North Pole became known as "Holmes' Hole." A 1901 Ohio newspaper wrote, "Men stand on the street and talk of the flying machine as an assured fact, and of a descent to Holmes' Hole not simply as a thing that is possible but as a very near probability." In the retelling, "Holmes" became some legendary captain who had (according to one 1913 account), "invented an aperture at the North Pole through which sucks the Gulf Stream, and which was called 'Holmes's hole.'"

Nobody has managed to dig very far below Vineyard Haven, but in the fall of 1976, Raymond Hall and a team from the US Geological Survey drilled an 860-foot borehole named "ENW-50" under the State Forest, in Edgartown, behind Dodgers Hole. The well penetrated one hundred million years of accumulated sedimentary strata, unearthing geological samples and pollen from the Cenomanian age, when dinosaurs roamed the surface, but stopped just short of the (theoretical) bedrock below. Fortunately, no Vernean shark-crocodiles or Ape Gigans emerged from Hall's hole.

A LAST FIT
OF INSANITY

Late one night in 1870, Edgartown boat builder Joseph Dunham threw his wife Angeline and their two daughters out of the house they owned near Tower Hill. He holed up there for the next three weeks, ignoring Angeline's pleas to return. When he finally invited her back, just as she was about to enter, Dunham shot her through the window, peppering her face, neck, and shoulder with forty or fifty shot. One pierced her windpipe, and her horrible wounds were feared to be fatal. Dunham was quickly captured. The *Vineyard Gazette* reported: "The sad result of this last fit of insanity on the part of Mr. Dunham, shows us plainly, how important it is that he be placed where he will never again put the life of any one in jeopardy. Every citizen of the community, should feel called upon by the wisest considerations of safety to person and property, to see that Joseph Dunham is never again permitted to have his freedom. If insane, let him be safely lodged in the Lunatic Asylum; if sane, justice and law, most assuredly, which he has outraged and set at defiance, should see that he is secured in some strong box, where the rays of light are not very brilliant."

Dunham had been an inmate at the Taunton Lunatic Asylum twice before, and he was soon returned to Taunton for his third and final stay. Angeline recovered, and soon sold the ancient Dunham homestead.

(The estate reportedly included an armchair given to the family by George Washington for some act of patriotism performed by one of his ancestors.) Dunham escaped twice from the asylum in Taunton over the next three years, but he was soon recaptured, and died in the asylum in 1875.

BAXTER'S SALOON

T. T. Baxter's Saloon was the front end of Baxter House, a seventy-five-guest hotel on Circuit Avenue next to the Island House—roughly where Carousel Ice Cream is today. Opened by Thatcher T. Baxter in 1868, it was one of the earliest hotels in Oak Bluffs. Baxter quickly tired of this venture and returned to his home in West Dennis in 1871, but the Baxter House continued under his name for many years afterward—first under J. & N. Phinney, then Gus Chase (formerly the head cook of the Central House), and by 1880 under A. B. Davis, who subsequently changed its name to Warwick House.

Baxter's "saloon" likely referred to an "ice cream saloon" rather than a bar, as liquor was still technically illegal here. (The Sea View and Highland House featured billiard and bowling "saloons" during the 1870s, as well.) "There is no drinking, no profanity (that I have heard), no rowdyism here . . . Nothing stronger than ginger ale is exposed for sale," wrote the *Hartford Courant* in 1872.

But that didn't mean that liquor was unavailable. Earlier that summer the *Courant* wrote of Oak Bluffs, "Liquor that intoxicates is not sold there; not even New England Rum, unless that may be the base of the 'Quaker Bitters,'" referring to the popular drugstore tonic that claimed to cure everything from pimples to worms to "female derangements." Another visiting Connecticut journalist wrote, "No spirituous liquors are sold in the place, yet you can find the contemptible 'Plantation Bit-

A thirteen-piece brass band poses on the porch above Baxter's Saloon on Circuit Avenue.

ters,' or in other words St. Croix rum, under the disguise of a few bitter drugs." (Plantation Bitters, like Quaker Bitters, were a druggist's cure for everything from constipation to mental despondency. "If the brain has been haunted by morbid fancies, they are out to flight" after a few bottles of the Quaker Bitters, read their claims.)

And it wasn't just the drugstores. In August 1879, Vermont contributor H.S.B. wrote in the *Burlington Free Press*:

> In the early days of its prosperity Martha's Vineyard was almost a synonym for sobriety and good order. Alas, that happy condi-

tion of things exists no longer. At every corner drug store and in the rear of nearly every boarding house liquors flow like water—provided they are paid for. While the Tabernacle is resounding with songs of praise, a dozen bar-rooms within a minute's walk echo the fiendish brawls of drunken sots.

Brass bands, however, were openly celebrated. A staple of summertime life in Cottage City, hotels joined forces to hire off-Island bands to play in town throughout the summer. The *New York Times* reported in 1885, "The hotel proprietors and others are negotiating for a band of 20 pieces to play here three times a day during the season and to enliven the warm Summer evenings with sweet lullabies."

THE NEPTUNE CLUB

The Neptune Club of Norwalk, Connecticut, was a yachting club, made up of wealthy businessmen from New York City and Connecticut, which made an annual excursion by schooner to Martha's Vineyard and Nantucket every summer throughout the 1860s, 1870s, and 1880s, usually forty or fifty members strong. After each cruise they published a "log book" of their adventures, mostly consisting of touring, fishing, and fine dining at fancy beachside resorts up the coast from Norwalk to Nantucket. Cottage City was a primary destination, where the club would stay a week or more each season. In 1875, they boasted of cruising from Norwalk to Oak Bluffs in a mere twenty-three hours.

"Commodore" Charles H. Tompkins, possibly the bearded gentleman in the lower right corner, was "commanding officer" of the Neptune Club for decades. A prominent national pricing expert in the wholesale drug trade, Tompkins oversaw the import, manufacture, and distribution of everything from aspirin and lettuce-extract powder to medicinal liquor, cannabis, opium, and heroin. His last firm, Schieffelin & Co., later dropped medicine altogether to become a major liquor distributor after Prohibition.

The Neptune Club of Norwalk, Connecticut, poses on the steps of their hotel in Oak Bluffs. [Photograph by Charles H. Shute & Son of Edgartown.]

1877: A gang of pickpockets and thieves struck the island over several days in late August. The Pawnee "suffered severely" after clothing and jewelry were stolen from its guests. Thieves entered a guest's room in the Sea View, picked the lock of her trunk, and stole $3,000 worth of diamonds. Nine people had their pockets picked near the Tabernacle, and one thief was caught attempting to steal a lady's watch near Clinton Avenue. [*Harrisburg Telegraph*]

PART II

THE 1880S

SHUGRUE

Timothy Shugrue of Newburyport was only eight years old when he was committed to reform school for larceny. A "natural thief" who had already been arrested several times for stealing, Shugrue had broken into a ship's chandlery and smashed open a desk with a hatchet to steal ten dollars. He "broke jail" once following his arrest, but was recaptured. And all before his ninth birthday.

His next five years consisted of alternating stints of residential reform school and short-term foster placements, until he was finally bound out to harness-maker R. W. Crocker of Vineyard Haven in 1876. His terms with Crocker were simple: clothing, schooling, and board for the first year, ten dollars salary the second year, and fifteen dollars the third year. In return, Shugrue was put to hard labor in Crocker's factory. Like many other teenage and preteen boys bound out to Crocker's harness factory over the years, Shugrue was overworked and physically abused. He was regularly whipped with a six-foot trace for minor offenses. But unlike most of the other boys, when Crocker's alleged crimes were finally brought to court, Shugrue ultimately testified for—rather than against—his boss in court, claiming that his whippings had all been deserved. Mr. Crocker, whom Gratia Harrington once remembered as "more or less the town boss" of Vineyard Haven, was ultimately exonerated in the eyes of the state and town officials, and so Shugrue found himself with a powerful friend.

Young Shugrue soon became involved in the town's cultural and charitable affairs. He became the bass drummer for the Vineyard Haven Band, and organized the parade for a new downtown water fountain. In 1890 he became secretary of the Royal Society of Good Fellows (a charitable fraternal order that met over what is now Leslie's Drug Store). He also became involved with the Ladies Library League of Vineyard Haven, which helped make the Vineyard Haven Public Library what it is today.

When Crocker's harness business failed, Shugrue attempted several times to start up his own Vineyard Haven business, including a men's clothing store, a laundry, and a small harness shop, but none of his enterprises lasted more than a couple of years. He was remembered best as the town's night watchman, lighting and maintaining the oil street lamps throughout the downtown area. He died in 1907 of kidney failure, at the untimely age of forty-four.

1881: "The ladies at Cottage City during the past few days reminded me very forcibly of the street costumes so frequently seen in the streets of Lima, for, as in Peru, these shrouded figures were more like pedestrian balloons than anything I can think of. But you can see the handsome faces of the wearers at Cottage City, while in Lima you can get only a glimpse of an eye roguishly turned toward the stranger. Sitting in a sheltered corner of the wide veranda I began calculating how many thousand dollars had been invested in rubber clothing, for every feminine form moving about was enveloped in its shiny and wavy folds, from the little girl of ten to the mature matron of I don't dare say how many years. No doubt $30,000 would be near the figure." [New York Herald]

THE COTTAGE CITY
CARNIVAL OF 1882

Illumination Night in the late nineteenth century was very different from the laid-back traditions Vineyarders enjoy today. During the 1870s and 1880s it took the form of an end-of-season blowout party celebrated across the whole of Oak Bluffs, known as the Cottage City Carnival.

The Carnival of Sports began in the afternoon, showcasing foot and bike races around Ocean Park for cash prizes, baseball games, three-legged and sack races, swimming contests (from Lovers Rock to the Sea View's pier), tennis matches, and whaleboat races. Professional athletes dove from seventy-foot-high platforms, walked tightropes, and performed trick bicycle stunts. In 1887, three thousand people gathered for a greased pig race on Ocean Avenue.

A highlight of the afternoon was always the half-mile obstacle race around Ocean Park, involving barrels to dive through, a greased pole to climb, a frisky horse to vault, hurdles, tilts, seven-foot fences, low wooden horses to squeeze under, a man to climb over, spiked barrels to navigate, and two ladders set on live horses' backs to walk over, rung by rung. It was known for its laughs as much as its athletics, but cash prizes were awarded to the winners. Meanwhile, the most popular bands from across the state arrived to play, often simultaneously, at

The finale set piece of the Carnival of 1882

various bandstands and parks across town. In 1880 an opera company performed in the park.

In this era just before electric lights arrived, the Grand Illumination encompassed all of Oak Bluffs at nightfall, as houses across town were hung with as many as six hundred Chinese and Japanese lanterns each, scattered throughout gardens and suspended from temporarily erected arches and artificial trees, together with long rows of torches, and candles in every window. Ocean and Circuit Avenues were the most brilliantly lit. Intense blue Bengal lights (used for signal flaring) and calcium lights (limelights) added to the intensity of the blaze, punctuated by homemade fireworks. Even yachts off shore were brilliantly decorated with lanterns.

Around 8:00 p.m. the grand torchlit procession began: an hour-long parade of brass bands, fire brigades, and decorated carriages making their way through two miles of Oak Bluffs streets, as homeowners ignited fireworks and launched paper "fire balloons." In 1875 the *Boston Globe* reported that the parade included "the robed advance guard of His Royal Highness, King Carnival, bearing battle axes," and noted that "the rest of the procession was made up of maskers in all sorts of characters." The 1884 parade was remembered for its torchlit parade of tricycles. Bringing up the end of the procession every year was the fireworks wagon, firing Roman candles and discharging flares and colored fires of all kinds as it traveled.

The procession ended at Ocean Park with a professional finale of aerial pyrotechnics: rockets, bombs, "dragon shells," sparkling jets, tourbillons, parachute rockets, and more, watched by as many as thirty thousand spectators, including senators, governors, generals, and even President Grant himself in 1874. An early display of Japanese fireworks by pyrotechnist M. Sato was followed in 1881 by a London artist who launched "a mammoth balloon carrying a powerful magnesium light and discharging fireworks." The grand finale each year was the discharge of a "set piece," typically a thirty-foot-high temple or triumphal arch wired with pyrotechnics, accompanied by hundreds of bombs, sky rockets, and Roman candles.

The 1882 Cottage City Carnival—the fifteenth annual—was typical of this era. The 1882 sports carnival involved a 240-yard dash between

"Miss Holmes of Holmes Hole, Miss Quick of Quick's Hole, and Miss Wood of Wood's Hole." The Grand Illumination included a pyramid of fire in Lake Anthony. The procession featured three bands and was followed by the fireworks chariot of Boston pyrotechnic company Masten & Wells. The mood was dampened slightly when the chariot's wheels crushed a seven-year-old boy named Carter, causing severe internal injuries, and when a horse, spooked by fireworks, inflicted a serious head injury to a woman on Narragansett Avenue, knocking her "insensible." Undeterred, the festivities continued at Ocean Park with four bands and three hours of heavy rockets and pyrotechnics, culminating in the discharge of the finale set piece, a massive sign, lit up in fire: "Welcome to Cottage City Carnival 1868–1882."

THE SILENT STEED

The 1880s was the decade of tricycling, and the massive three-wheelers of this era were no children's toys. A tricycling craze, started in England, held summer visitors to the Island completely in its grips for more than a decade, as bicycle and tricycle races became part of Cottage City's annual "carnival of athletic sports" in the weeks leading up to the final Illumination. At least one tricycle rental shop—sometimes referred to as the "tricycle stable"—was located prominently on Circuit Avenue.

One newspaper reporter observed in July 1885, "The number of bicycles and tricycles which have been brought to the Vineyard this season is simply enormous. Several hundred machines are already in use on the Island, and more are arriving by every boat. Nearly every young fellow in town has brought his wheel with him, and tricycling is fast coming into favour with the ladies. The roads here, being entirely of concrete, furnish excellent opportunities for the use of the machines, and the riders of the silent steeds fully appreciate this fact." Another Cottage City visitor added in 1887, "Tricycle riding seems to be very popular with the ladies. The concrete streets are delightful for such exercise and a dozen or more ladies may be seen at almost any time in the morning or early evening gliding through the streets. Each carries a colored light in the evening and as the riders go darting around the effect is a pretty one."

While most popular with women, it was not exclusively so. In the summer of 1887, three famous international oarsmen—famed previously for their sculling rather than their tricycling—squared off in a memorable ten-mile race: 140 laps around the Cottage City Casino in "rowing tricycles"—a sort of recumbent three-wheeler also referred to as the "roadsculler." Rowers Wallace Ross, George Hosmer, and John McKay launched their tricycles in front of a large Vineyard crowd to vie for the three-hundred-dollar prize. Ross was declared the winner, and entered the record books for having rowed the "almost incredible distance of ten miles in thirty-nine minutes" on his tricycle.

ALEXANDER GRAHAM BELL'S EXTRAORDINARY PHENOMENON

Alexander Graham Bell, known best for the invention of the tele-phone, wrote a letter in 1885 to his wife Mabel about an inves-tigation he undertook while visiting Vineyard Haven, after hearing an unusual story from the local Unitarian minister, Rev. Daniel W. Stevens of the Sailors Reading Room on Hatch Road. He wrote:

> [An] extraordinary phenomenon [the Rev. Stevens] told me about. It seems that on the 10th of October last about 3 o'clock in the afternoon, his grandson Waldo (a boy of about 13 or 14) was picking cranberries with a party of others occupied in the same way—at a cranberry marsh about a mile and a half away when the whole party were startled by a loud volcanic sort of rumbling sound from the ground near them—followed by a Natural Flood—Rock-explosion sort of effect. A mass of water—estimated as about the diameter of a large dining room table—in the middle of a neighbouring pond was thrown up into the air to a height of 10 or twelve feet. I cross-questioned a man—a Mr. Cleveland, who was an eyewitness and heard other versions. His story tallied with that of the boy's. The water

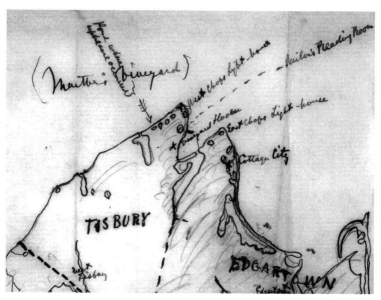

Part of a map drawn by Alexander Graham Bell for his wife. An arrow in the upper left is labelled "Pond where upheaval occurred."

immediately subsided, leaving a cloud like steam over the spot which gradually drifted away and "dissolved into thin air" like Shakespeare's ghost. Huge circular ripples seemingly several inches above the general surface of the water appeared on the pond, and after a little general disturbance all was quiet again. Mrs. Cleveland, the wife of my informant, thought that immediately after the upheaval the level of the surface in the middle of the pond was lower than at the edges, but her husband did not think so—nor did there appear any change of level that could be observed. The cause of this upheaval—which is quite unprecedented on the Island—is a mystery. The circumstance has not yet been brought to the attention of any Scientific man capable of judging, but it appears to me it should be investigated.

On Sunday afternoon Mr. Stevens drove me to the spot, where we were joined by Mr. Cleveland and Waldo. I had the benefit of hearing the story again upon the spot—but the phenomenon appears as inexplicable as at first. I wonder if Major Powell would be the man to inform. It should certainly be investigated. I have indicated the little pond where the upheaval occurred upon the map by an arrow head. It is on the farm of Mr. Alexander Smith.

What caused this mysterious phenomenon (likely corresponding to the modern body of water sometimes known as Wilfrid's Pond)?

Dr. Maurice Tivey, marine geologist at the Woods Hole Oceanographic Institution, speculates that it may have been a "methane gas expulsion event." Rare in southern New England, it could still occur if the pond had "significant organic material that was buried under an impermeable cap of clay that failed and released the built-up gas."

THE WOODEN LEG

William Cunningham of Boston was barely ten years old when he was sent to reform school in 1870 for "larceny and disobedience." His parents were alcoholics, the family was destitute and sometimes homeless, and William had run away regularly for weeks at a time. Two years into his stay at the State Reform School at Westborough, he suffered an accident with a mowing machine and lost his leg. (He would later claim he was crippled in a heroic act stopping a team of horses.)

Just before his fourteenth birthday Cunningham was "bound out" to Rodolphus Crocker of Vineyard Haven to learn the harness-making trade. Crocker took in many wards of the state, both from the State Primary School at Monson and the State Reform School, and his crew of "Monson boys" made up a large part of his sizable workforce.

Cunningham quickly soured to Island life. According to his state files, Cunningham was initially "quarrelsome and discontented," and got into "rows" with the other boys. He was caught stealing tobacco, and Crocker wouldn't let him attend school that winter "on account of his disposition." But neither Crocker nor the state authorities would allow him to leave, even as Cunningham wrote imploring letters to state authorities stating he was "dissatisfied and wants to be taken away." It was later testified that Crocker "thrashed" him and that "he preferred the reform school to Crocker." But as the years passed, his complaints became more tempered, and eventually ended.

Crocker's Harness Factory in July 1884, now the location of the stone bank in Vineyard Haven. Twenty-four-year-old William Cunningham stands with the "Monson Boys" and other factory employees.

When Cunningham turned sixteen, he requested an artificial leg to replace his old wooden stump. State authorities balked at the enormous cost (nearly one hundred dollars), but Mr. H. Levin of Vineyard Haven and a group of local "ladies"—probably with the Vineyard Haven Baptist Church, in which Cunningham had become involved—began a fundraising campaign, and in a special act of the Massachusetts legislature the state agreed to contribute matching funds. In early 1878 he was fitted with his new Palmer Artificial Leg, which Cunningham declared "perfectly satisfactory."

Upon turning eighteen, Cunningham continued on as a professional workman with Crocker. He married Winnie Smith of Vineyard Haven, the daughter of highly respected town leaders, and they had two children. "Happily married. Keeping house. Respected by everybody," reads the end of his file, made by the state visiting agent in 1881 before closing his case.

But his story didn't end so happily.

In 1884, in what the *Boston Globe* called "about the only scandal that ever shocked the town," it was charged that Crocker had abused, beaten, and overworked his boys, keeping them as "virtual prisoners." It was even alleged that Crocker's friend, the Vineyard Haven postmaster, had intercepted outgoing complaint letters. But Cunningham defended his boss, and denied all the allegations of abuse. The charges against Crocker were eventually dropped, and Cunningham soon became superintendent of the harness factory.

Cunningham's marriage failed next. Winnie alleged he choked, kicked, and tried to cut her throat in "insanely jealous" fits, and that he threatened to shoot her father with the twin bulldog revolvers he carried (and practiced shooting with on prowling cats). He was arrested, but the charges were evidently dropped. They were divorced about 1888.

Cunningham left the Island and moved to Boston, temporarily finding work with a Charlestown harness-maker. He met a twenty-year-old Welsh "domestic" named Maggie Williams, and they soon became engaged. He didn't tell her about his artificial leg, nor when he lost his new job.

THE SCENE IN MRS. SOLOMON'S PARLOR, WHERE THE SHOOTING OCCURRED.

Boston Post *illustration, published April 26, 1892*

One day he slipped on the sidewalk and broke his Vineyard-bought leg. Lacking the funds to pay for a new one —or his rent—Cunningham stayed in bed for two weeks, pretending to be healing from a broken bone. He borrowed Maggie's gold watch and ring, and twenty-two dollars, and (using a borrowed crutch) secretly went out and bought a new leg, then quietly moved out of his room without paying his back rent. His ruse fell apart when Maggie went to visit and instead discovered the truth from his angry landlord. She became incensed by all of his deceptions, but particularly about his secret wooden leg. Their upcoming wedding was canceled.

On the morning of April 25, 1892, Cunningham arranged for a reconciliatory meeting with Maggie at the home of their mutual friend Mrs. Solomon in Cambridgeport. On his way to meet her, he purchased a .32-caliber Colt revolver, and then stopped into a neighborhood pharmacy to have his knee oiled. They met, he begged her forgiveness, she refused, and he shot her twice, and then himself. She died on the way to the hospital, but Cunningham eventually recovered. Newspapers as far away as California picked up the story over the next few days, as Cunningham pled not guilty on the grounds that an accident occurred when he was trying to intimidate her, or alternately that she "got in his way while he was trying to commit suicide." He eventually withdrew his plea and pled guilty to second-degree murder. He was sentenced to the State Prison for life.

Twenty years later, in 1912, Governor Eugene Foss pardoned Cunningham. His lawyer picked him up at the prison gate, and in the first automobile ride of his life he drove to the State House to thank the governor for his freedom. His whereabouts afterward are unknown. His two Vineyard-born children moved to Oak Bluffs and changed their names.

CHICK'S VINEYARD
HAVEN NEWS

When Edson Chick arrived on the Vineyard in the summer of 1887, Islanders found him to be charismatic, well spoken, impeccably dressed, and extremely outgoing. A man of unusual intelligence, Chick attracted attention and friends wherever he went. He was a wealthy and distinguished writer and journalist, a talented musician and showman, and he was about to publish Vineyard Haven's first real newspaper, *Chick's Vineyard Haven News*.

What Vineyarders didn't know was that Edson Chick was also a committed maniac who had escaped from his last insane asylum by picking the lock with a tool he had made from his toothbrush. Rearrested and released, but unwelcomed at home by his wife and children, Chick's half-brother agreed to pay him a weekly pension to go live in a quiet place "to be kept away from a big city": Martha's Vineyard.

Chick's newspaper was published from October 1887 until March 1888 out of an office in Lane's Block, where Leslie's Drug Store is today. It was an immediate hit. He became a dedicated local journalist, carefully and accurately (if often colorfully) following the stories of the day, including local politics, gossip, and pointed editorial commentary. Chick gushed over the Island, the town, and most of its industrious

CHICK'S
VINEYARD HAVEN NEWS.

[Entered at the Post Office, Vineyard Haven, as Second Class Matter.]

GO WORK IN THE VINEYARD.

VOL. 1, NO. 4.   NOVEMBER 17, 1887.   PRICE 2 CENTS.

The November 17, 1887, edition of Chick's newspaper

inhabitants, contrasting it with "the cold shores of distant America." He printed his motto, "Go Work in the Vineyard," in the masthead.

Chick suffered from a debilitating form of bipolar disorder—known in the 1880s as "circular insanity"—and had been institutionalized a half-dozen times before coming to the Island. *The Brooklyn Eagle* wrote about Chick and his Vineyard newspaper, "There was nothing the matter with him except a slight ailment which Philistines called 'rats in his garret.' Now and then one of these mental 'rats' would escape and run across the editorial page of his paper, to the wonder of the rural readers whose respect for Mr. Chick's profundity prevented their suspecting that anything was wrong with him."

His paper was full of playful and insightful (if sometimes sarcastic and troublemaking) wordplay. Under the *Vineyard Haven* column "Points":

> "A cyclone of fair clerks, crowds of customers, and a beautiful array of tempting goods sweeps over Frank P. Norton's store. One can't help buying of Nobby-Tasty-Tidy-Fly-Brushed-Off-Frank."

Under a regular column titled "Thinks":

"In a store here, a man said that some coffee he bought 'tasted like ground-up shoe taps and state religion.' He knows his name. We forgot it."

Chick's newspaper, which he claimed to print more than a thousand copies of each week, lasted less than twenty-five issues. He ran out of money, and his printer refused to publish the paper without further payment. Unable to pay his bill at the Mansion House, Chick left the Island and was forced to leave all of his clothes at the hotel for board.

1887: "Mr. T. Shugrue while sober and damp on last Thursday night, went for his umbrella. His umbrella was in the ditch. Much mud ensued." [*Chick's Vineyard Haven News*]

SUMMER TOBOGGANS, THE CASINO, AND THE NORTH BLUFF FLYING HORSES

The Flying Horses, the Casino, and the Summer Toboggan Coast are clustered in the background of this late-1880s view down Kennebec Avenue toward North Bluff, as photographed from the top of the old Metropolitan Hotel (near the present post office). The Highland Wharf is visible in the distance on the left just a short walk down the beach, with Lake Anthony (now Oak Bluffs Harbor) on the far left.

The Flying Horses appears here in its original location on North Bluff, behind the vast Casino, and not far from where the Lookout Tavern is today. The origins of the Flying Horses have never been conclusively determined, but evidence suggests that they were built about 1876, probably at Coney Island, but they were moved to Oak Bluffs in the summer of 1884. The Cottage City correspondent for the *Fitchburg Sentinel* reported that summer, "A new building, dubbed with the high sounding name of 'The Carousel,' has been erected near the Skating rink, in which are flying horses for the amusement of the children and sometimes for 'children of a larger growth.'" (The massive Casino, which could house more than fifteen hundred people at one time, was

View of the Flying Horses at North Bluff, circa 1887

originally built as a roller skating rink. But in 1886 it was retrofitted with a stage and scenery and renamed "the Casino.")

The official 1887 program for "Three Gala Days at Cottage City"—a town-wide event that culminated in the Grand Illumination and the Fireworks—kicked off with a morning baseball game between the Cottage Citys and the New Bedfords, and was reportedly held at "Toboggan Park"—presumably the empty field to the left of the toboggan slide. A "trotting track" was also remembered as being located here about this time.

A series of gales struck the Island during the winter of 1888–89, the worst of which is sometimes simply called "the Gale of 1888." The violent late-November nor'easter was the extratropical remnants of a late-season Category 2 hurricane that swept the coast from New Jersey to Maine. "The Massachusetts coast is lined with wrecks," reported the *New York Times*. Four schooners parted their anchors and were driven ashore on the Island, including the *Lizzie Young* of Boston, which was blown ashore south of Cottage City.

The *New York Times* reported from Cottage City the following summer: "Summer visitors this year will witness the fearful results of last Winter's storms, which visited this island with nearly as much impetuosity as they did Coney Island and the Jersey coast. The bluff on which the plank walk rested for over half a mile from the Sea View House to Cluster Village has been eaten into from twenty to thirty feet and the walk destroyed. In its place the town has built a strong bulkhead with a graded embankment, but the loss of the promenade will be seriously felt. The carousel that stood next to the Casino has been moved from the sea front to safer quarters near the main street, and the toboggan slide is a thing of memory."

In hindsight, the move was a very lucky break for the Flying Horses. The Casino burned down three years later, in September 1892, together with the Seaview hotel and a number of other neighboring buildings. "A southwest wind is all that saved the town" reported the papers—the same wind that would have almost certainly spread the inferno to the Flying Horses to the north, had it still been located there.

1887: Vineyard Haven's water system was formally opened in a huge celebration. Main Street merchants decorated their stores with colorful buntings as a large crowd turned out in a steady afternoon rain to see an exhibition of the downtown hydrants. A hose was attached to the town's first hydrant, and water thrown over all three stories of both Crocker's harness factory and Lane's Block. It got a little out of hand. The *Martha's Vineyard Herald* reported, "The turning of the stream from hydrant directly upon a spectator a few yards distant was not a handsome thing to do." That evening, 250 guests gathered at the Association Hall, which had been hung with dozens of Chinese and Japanese lanterns. Music was performed and speeches were made, including one by John Quincy Adams Brackett, lieutenant governor of Massachusetts. The feast of turkey, oysters, and lobster salad lasted until morning.

THE JOGGINS

It emerged from a heavy fog into Vineyard Haven Harbor just after midnight on August 8, 1888. It was nearly an eighth of a mile long, and described as "cigar shaped," crowned by a half-dozen large lights. "It is simply enormous," wrote the *New York Herald*. More than twice the length of the modern M.V. *Island Home*, "the *Joggins*" (as it was informally known) measured 592 feet in length, but had no propulsion or steering.

It was claimed at the time to be the largest raft ever constructed. Composed of twenty-four thousand logs, mostly spruce, from the Bay of Fundy, it was fifty-five feet wide and bound with forty-five miles of wire, cable, and chains. Like a wooden iceberg, two-thirds of the *Joggins* lay below the water's surface. A crew of half a dozen men looked after the hawsers and lights as it was pulled by two of the most powerful tugs in the country, *Underwriter* and *Ocean King*. It was a radical new method to transport lumber; the *Joggins* moved the equivalent of forty-five lumber schooners full of timber at a substantially lower cost.

The *Joggins*'s owner and architect was James Leary, a New York City shipbuilder and contractor. A loyal Tammany Hall man, he held multiple municipal contracts for large public-works projects in and around the city. (He would soon earn fame as the builder of New York's Harlem River Drive.)

Eight days after its launch from Joggins, Nova Scotia, Leary's log raft stopped in Vineyard Haven to coal and water the two tugs on their

Vineyarders pose atop the Joggins, *August 8, 1888, in Vineyard Haven Harbor. [Photograph by Joseph N. Chamberlain.]*

ten-day adventure down the coast. The raft's speed averaged about three knots. It drew attention all the way down, but nothing like the reception it received on the Vineyard. Captain F. J. Riley of the *Underwriter* reported to the New York press, "You should have seen the crowds at Vineyard Haven. Thousands boarded her. She was black with human beings. Old and young men and women and girls came out in rowboats to get a sight of the concern." Captain Riley told a second paper, "At Vineyard Haven at least 5,000 people surrounded us in boats or climbed up on the logs. The women were as eager to see our raft as the men, and came aboard by hundreds."

The *Joggins* was not Leary's first attempt to deliver logs via raft from the Maritime Provinces to New York. One year earlier, in 1887, Leary hired the steamer *Miranda* to tow a 560-foot spruce raft consisting of twenty-seven thousand logs to the city. Similar in construction to the *Joggins*, the raft was described as resembling a "caterpillar going along humping its back." Unlike the second voyage, their course took the raft south of the Island. But forty-five miles south of Chappaquiddick, they were forced to abandon it in a fierce gale directly in the track of European ships approaching New York and Philadelphia. Alarms were raised on both sides of the Atlantic, and the US Navy sent out vessels to locate the dangerously drifting and disintegrating lost raft. A week later, a "great mass of logs" was located off Nantucket, visible as far as the eye could see. The newspapers described it as "a Sargasso Sea of logs." The six-mile-wide field of floating timber gradually floated north on the Gulf Stream, slowly dispersing, and was regularly sighted even years later as far away as Greenland and the Azores.

The *Joggins* left Vineyard Haven before noon, and crossing through Vineyard Sound, reached New York successfully two days later, passing through Hell Gate and under the Brooklyn Bridge with the aid of a half a dozen tugs. Most of the logs are said to have found their final destination as lowland fill for the immense Astor estate along the Harlem River in Upper Manhattan.

Two years later, Leary brought a second, even longer raft to Vineyard Haven, putting into the harbor on August 1, 1890, to avoid bad weather. His new raft consisted of seven thousand pine logs, stretching more than one thousand feet in length in seventeen sections, and was described by the *New York Sun* as "hitched tandem, like the joints of a backbone . . . suggesting the back of an enormous dislocated sea snake."

1889: William Benson of Chilmark was arrested for the attempted murder of his father, West Tisbury farmer David Benson, and stepmother, Orinda, by putting Paris Green (a highly toxic rodenticide) and arsenic in their eel chowder and in David's whiskey. He gave a confession, which he later denied giving, in which he tried to implicate his stepmother in the plot. "William has been a thorn in the flesh of the aged parent for a long time," noted the *Boston Globe*, "The residents of Tisbury believe William guilty of the awful charge, and say it was a common expression of the young man's when about leaving company that he guessed 'he would go home and see if the old man had croked.'"

PART III

THE 1890S

THE METROPOLITAN

Cottage City's Metropolitan Hotel, which once commanded a central location on Circuit Avenue occupied today by the Corner Store, advertised seventy-five "large airy rooms and pleasant piazzas" together with excellent meals and the occasional "straw ride" to West

Modern Oak Bluffs almost seems like a small country town when you compare it with the metropolis that was Cottage City. These three grand seasonal hotels—from left to right, the Pawnee House, the Metropolitan Hotel, and the Oakwood—once dominated the center of town, where today stands Eastaway, the Corner Store, and Phillips Hardware.

Chop. During its heyday in the late 1880s and 1890s, it shared management with its neighboring hotel across Park Avenue, the Pawnee. Its ground floor was occupied for decades by Norton's Pharmacy and Rausch's ice cream parlor (serving "original Vienna ice cream").

The top stories of Pawnee House were removed in the mid-1950s, and its first floor survives today. On the other side of the Metropolitan, the hotel Oakwood was also radically shortened and extensively renovated. But the grand Metropolitan, which continued serving as a hotel into the Depression era, was destroyed by a fire in the late 1930s or early 1940s, and the modern one-story Corner Store building was built in its place shortly afterward.

1890: "It is a fixed idea in the native mind that Capt. Kidd buried gold on Chappaquiddick. I suppose not a youngster that ever grew up on the island has not dug for gold. There is a huge elephantine-backed rock, near one of the Coast Survey marks, that looks as if it ought to have some business there. There is not a rod of ground about this rock that has not been turned up and down to the sea level. There is a tradition that forty feet below the surface is an inscription, and, of course, cut by Capt. Kidd." [New York Evening Post]

DRINKING, SMOKING, LODGING, AND FISH

A quiet moment on the stretch of Circuit Avenue between the Island House and the Arcade building during the late 1880s or early 1890s.

A pair of high-wheeled bicycles rest in front of the Cottage City House, the summer hotel owned and operated for many years by Mrs. Sarah Stearns. Well known for her hospitality and homemade bread, Mrs. Stearns kept a second hotel in Florida during the colder months. Her husband William, an off-Island railroad superintendent, was remembered for having helped escort President Lincoln, in disguise, from Philadelphia to Washington after his election.

Slightly hidden from view, next to the barber pole, is the Globe Fish Market, run by Louis A. Pease of Edgartown. His son Ernest, who clerked here for many years, later opened an ice business.

The G.D. Dows & Co. store at the center was a branch store of the Boston bottling company that pioneered carbonated drinks in the United States. The Dows company claimed to be the first bottler of carbonated ginger ale in the country, and was also well known for its bottled Jamaica ginger cordials (presumably alcoholic) and "champagne ginger," as well as its fruit juices, extracts, and mineral and soda waters. The signs in this photo suggest that beer and cigars may also have been popular with the Cottage City summertime crowd.

Circuit Avenue, Cottage City

1891: Former state senator Howes Norris of Vineyard Haven, and editor Charles Strahan of the *Martha's Vineyard Herald*, exchanged a volley of increasingly nasty public letters over politics, in which Strahan called Norris "a peanut salesman" and a "sneak," and Norris declared himself "not afraid to meet you on the stump, in print, or in the field." This last phrase suggested to the *Boston Globe* that the first high-profile duel in decades was about to be fought, and went as far as publishing all twenty-six rules of the traditional English dueling code on the front page of the newspaper, and suggesting West Tisbury as the best site for the fight.

FRANK PERRY'S SEGAR STORE

Cigar maker Frank Perry (1848–1913) emigrated to the United States as a teenager from the island of São Jorge (St. George) in the Azores. He learned cigar making very early in life—perhaps on his native island—and made a career of satisfying the growing American appetite for cigars. Arriving on Martha's Vineyard in the mid-1870s, he opened a "segar store" in the newly built Arcade building on Circuit Avenue, where he sold imported and domestic cigars, snuff, chewing tobacco, "smokers articles," as well as a full line of walking sticks. The tobacco brands he stocked included "Solace," "Gail & Ax's," "Vanity Fair," "Gem," and "Bagley's May Flower." Perry maintained his shop here for over thirty years, and by the end of his life was considered among the most prominent Azorean citizens of Oak Bluffs. Photographer Shute sold a series of 3-D views of Martha's Vineyard for stereoscope-wielding tourists, and his view of Perry's store was featured as an important Oak Bluffs landmark. Today, the Arcade building houses Sharky's Cantina and Big Al's, and continues to serve as the gateway to the Campgrounds. It is listed on the National Register of Historic Places.

Half of a stereoscopic photograph published by R. G. Shute of Edgartown in the 1880s or 1890s, captioned "Frank J. Perry's Segar Store, Arcade Building, Oak Bluffs."

FIVE MOTHERS, FIVE BABIES

Five Vineyard Haven moms pose with their kids about 1890. From left: Mrs. Margaret (Soule) Hough and her daughter, Doris Hough; Mrs. Juliet (Crocker) Merry and her son, Rodolphus Merry; Mrs. Fannie (Lewis) Look and her son, Ralph Look; Mrs. Annie (Daggett) Lord and her daughter, Constance Lord; and Mrs. Jennie (Cromwell) Clough and her son, Clifton Clough. Clifton's father, Charles Clough, was a professional photographer, and may have been the artist behind the camera.

EAT, SLEEP AND MEDITATE

"What a place Martha's Vineyard would have been to the late Sancho Panza for his morning snoozes," remarked a cigar-smoking Cottage City visitor, sitting with his feet resting high upon a railing and overheard by a *Boston Globe* reporter in 1890—"I

A quiet moment in Cottage City

declare I haven't done anything but eat and sleep since I came here, three days ago."

In a gossipy piece titled "Cottage City Snoozes. The Guests Eat, Sleep and Meditate," the *Globe* reporter concluded, "It seems as if the only object in life at such a resort as Cottage City is to eat, sleep, and smoke . . . there surely is something in the air about these regions which is totally demoralizing to wakefulness and energy. It might also be added, truthfully, that most of the summer sojourners take very kindly to this sort of listless life, so unlike the hurly-burly of the work-a-day world."

THE TINMAN

For nearly fifty years, Charles Mayhew ran a popular Edgartown hardware business, selling stoves, plumbing supplies, dishes, kettles, keys, cinder shovels, pumps, pipes, wire, pots and pans, glassware, and even a few groceries from his shop on the corner of North Water and Winter Streets in Edgartown. He usually referred to himself as a "tinman" or "tinsmith," although he once yearned for more precious metals.

When the discovery of gold in California was announced in 1848, twenty-one-year-old Mayhew and a couple dozen of his friends hastily formed the Edgartown Mining Company. Hiring the ship *Walter Scott*, they left the Island on May 7, 1849, on a 156-day journey to San Francisco. But like most of the Vineyard's forty-niners (more than two hundred from Edgartown alone), Mayhew soon came home, none the richer from his adventure. Shortly after he returned, he opened his downtown tinware shop, which the *Boston Globe* would later describe as a "more or less lucrative business," and Mayhew as "among the most energetic business spirits of the port."

A staunch Democrat, Mayhew was disheartened when Republican candidate Rutherford Hayes was elected president in the hotly disputed 1876 election. A Pennsylvania newspaper reported, "Charles Mayhew, of Edgartown, Massachusetts, has made a bet which stamps him as a fool. He has agreed to crawl from Edgartown to Oak Bluffs on his hands and knees if Hayes is elected. It is unnecessary to say that

Mayhew's tinware shop, on the corner of North Water and Winter Streets, circa 1890s. Charles Mayhew (1826–1910), seated left.

Mayhew is a Democrat, and that he is now seeking some means to rob his self-imposed task of its most ridiculous and disagreeable features." It was not reported whether Mayhew ultimately made good on his bet.

Mayhew and his family lived in his ancestral waterfront home on South Water Street, commonly referred to as the Governor Mayhew House. Built possibly as early as 1670, and occupied by many generations of Mayhews, it was widely considered the oldest house on the Island before it was unceremoniously torn down upon Charles Mayhew's death in 1910.

WHEELMEN AT THE CASINO

Gathering on an Island once known more for whalemen than wheelmen, the Massachusetts division of the League of American Wheelmen (LAW) mug with their bikes outside the Casino in Cottage City. Each summer during the 1880s and 1890s some five hundred bicycle enthusiasts from all over New England gathered here for road racing and coasting contests. "Cottage City has over 40 miles of concrete pavement," remarked the *New York Times* in 1894, "and thus affords better wheeling than any city in the country except Washington." On the back of this photograph is inscribed the phrase "Hickory Hall"—a reference to an Oak Bluffs bicycle establishment run in the early 1890s by Richmond Stoehr, better known by his trick bike riding stage name "Dick Alden," who may have been the local organizer of this event.

Built originally as a roller skating rink on the corner of Sea View and Oak Bluffs Avenues (about where the bank is today), this massive building was retrofitted with a stage and scenery in 1886 and renamed "the Casino"—effectively creating a convention hall worthy of every organization from the LAW to the "Pleasure Seekers' Social Engagement Club." On July 4, 1887, fifteen hundred people (or by some newspaper reports, five thousand people) gathered at the Casino to hear

The Cottage City Casino

international religious superstar Rev. Dr. DeWitt Talmage of Brooklyn give his oration, while "profuse decorations of flags, banners, and Chinese lanterns swayed in the breeze."

The Casino burned down in September 1892, together with the Sea View Hotel and a number of other neighboring buildings. "A southwest wind is all that saved the town," reported the papers. The LAW still exists today as the League of American Bicyclists.

THE MAKONIKEY

In July 1893, the *Boston Globe* reported the opening of a new hotel on Martha's Vineyard "called by the ultra-fashionable name of Makonikey inn, which is situated on the highest ground of Makonikey hights." A corruption of the Wampanoag name "Conaconaket" ("ancient place"), Makonikey marks an ancient boundary dividing the area once known as Chickemmoo, and today marks the town line between Tisbury and West Tisbury on the north shore. Surrounded by rich clay deposits, it was the site of a brick kiln in 1700.

The fancy new three-story hotel, funded by a syndicate of off-Island capitalists, featured twenty rooms, four dining salons, and a laundry. A bathhouse offered guests a choice of fresh- or saltwater bathing in porcelain tubs, in addition to an expansive beach on the shore below. It was the first hotel on the Island with an electrical generator, and each room was equipped with its own electric light. Four or five cottages were built on a labyrinth of newly graded roads, and lots for another two hundred were put up for sale. A two-hundred-foot wharf met guests debarking steamboats from Woods Hole and West Chop, and a survey was even drawn up for a new road to connect Makonikey directly to West Chop.

The opening was a grand success. The hotel hired the Boston Ladies' Banjo, Mandolin and Guitar Club for the season's entertainment—an ensemble led by Mrs. Helen Friend-Robinson on the banjeaurine, banjo, mandolin, and guitar, and featuring child prodigy Maudie Scott.

But 1893 turned out to be a terrible time to open a hotel. The economic crisis known as the "Panic of 1893" crippled the national economy, and when the time came five weeks after the hotel opened to pay the sixteen Italian workers from New Bedford who had just finished grading the hotel grounds, the contractor who hired them skipped town. Out of both money and food, the workers stormed and occupied the lobby of the new hotel, and threatened to burn it down unless payment was forthcoming. It wasn't. The guests panicked.

Henry Beetle Hough, in his 1936 book *Martha's Vineyard Summer Resort* described the scene: "In the still darkness, a file of frightened people emerged from the hotel and took flight toward Vineyard Haven, some of them partly dressed, some dragging suitcases and other belongings, some leaving almost everything behind. Their ankles torn by briars and bushes, the guests cut across fields and through thickets, not pausing to feel out paths or roads. The stragglers reached Vineyard Haven at last and were received and sheltered." They departed on the morning boat. Meanwhile, the furious workmen refused to leave.

The Makonikey Inn opened and closed in 1893.

"Italian Workmen at Makonikey Hights Demand Their Pay or the Blood of Their Employers" read the headline in the *Boston Globe* the next day. The hotel keeper, George Q. Pattee of Somerville, hired eight armed men from Cottage City as a private police force to guard himself, and a handful of (also unpaid) servants from the mob of angry men who spoke almost no English. Tension was abated somewhat as Pattee's servants fed the workers from the hotel kitchen. "The sympathies of the people around the town are altogether with the unpaid employees," reported the *Globe*, noting that the workers lacked the funds to even leave the Island.

While the end of the standoff was not reported, it was a death knell for the hotel. It may have reopened briefly under new management the next summer, but it never found its footing again. In 1897 it was sold at auction. From 1913 until 1919 the YMCA used the aging premises as a summer camp, and during the Great Depression, squatters were said to have taken residence in the abandoned hotel building. In 1932 a party of young people sailed over from Woods Hole to play "murder in a haunted house," only to be detained by the State Police to face charges of destruction of property. (They paid seven hundred dollars in a settlement.) The building was still (mostly) standing as late as 1936.

Over the years the cottages were sold and moved, and the hotel was slowly dismantled by neighbors and opportunists. Lawyer Charles Brown is said to have purchased a number of the cottages and moved them to Vineyard Haven, where many still stand today. Nothing remains of the Makonikey today but a few traces of the foundation and, it's reported, a couple of porcelain bathtubs.

1893: The *Vineyard Gazette* announced "Telephonic Communication with Mainland." George Hough, city editor of the *New Bedford Standard*, and US weather observer William Neifert of Vineyard Haven, spoke by long-distance telephone—the Island's first such conversation. Neifert had proposed the experiment to attach the government wire in his office to a long distance transmitter, while the telegraph operator at Buzzard's Bay connected the telegraph wire to the Southern Massachusetts Telephone Company's circuit. Railroad operator Mr. Bowley in Buzzards Bay assisted by connecting one wire of the New Bedford metallic circuit with the telegraph line from the Vineyard. The telegraph line extended overland from Vineyard Haven to Gay Head, where it connected with a submarine cable crossing Vineyard Sound to Pasque, then to Naushon, then to Woods Hole, and then to New Bedford via Buzzards Bay. The newspaper reported, "For the first time the voice of a man in New Bedford was heard on the Island."

THE DANZELL SISTERS

A series of devastating arson cases terrified Cottage City residents during the mid-1890s, culminating in the destruction of the Cottage City schoolhouse and five cottages on Clinton Avenue in 1894. Fire insurance companies began to refuse coverage in town, and a reward was offered to catch the "firebugs."

A Vineyard Haven day laborer named Daniel Lewis, arrested on charges of theft and incendiarism in Cottage City, implicated a young woman named Julia Danzell in a statement made to Sheriff Dexter. "They went to the front of a small cottage which was near the corner and sat on the grass, Julia sitting on his knee," reported the *Boston Globe*. "She had a cigarette and asked for a match. She then got up and walked to the rear of the building, Lewis following her. She pulled some grass, lit it with the match, and placed it under the shingles of the house. Lewis says he asked her what she would do now, and Julia replied: 'None of your business. I had a spite with a man.'"

Stolen items from the cottages were soon found in the possession of both Julia and her sister Lulu, and the sisters were charged with breaking-and-entering as well as larceny and arson. Their cases dragged on for years in court, and one of the sisters died in prison in 1900.

THE NAUMKEAG

With a capacity of two hundred guests, the Hotel Naumkeag was among the largest in Cottage City, and at three dollars a night, it was among the priciest as well. It stood for more than half a century on the corner of Narragansett and Naumkeag Avenues, about two blocks from Ocean Park, where today lies a close-knit residential neighborhood in the heart of Oak Bluffs. Opened about 1886 by Fred Lane, the Naumkeag advertised "electric bells and gas in all the rooms" as well as a "delicate and varied cuisine." The large dining room was regularly cleared and decorated with wildflower wreaths and Chinese lanterns, and dance "hops" were held for hotel guests and their invited friends.

The Naumkeag overcame a bad start: One predawn morning in August 1887 a professional safecracker came calling and stole five hundred dollars in cash and an eight-hundred-dollar diamond pin, the property of guests, as well as cleaning out eighty-six dollars from the hotel's cash drawer.

But it was an incident at the Naumkeag a few years later, in August 1894, which drew the attention of the Boston press. About midnight, guests were awakened by shouting and cries for help on the third floor. The night watchman rushed frantically through the building to locate the source of the trouble. "The guests by this time had found their way to the corridors in terror, thinking the house must be on fire or some

The Hotel Naumkeag, Cottage City

murder foul being committed," reported the *Boston Globe*. (The hotel had only that season complied with a police inspector's order to install rope fire-escapes, but evidently they were not employed that night.) The *Globe* reporter continued, "Finally the room from which the terrible cries proceeded was found, and the watchman pounded on the door of No. 21, shouting to the disturber of the peace to 'wake up.' It was learned that Mr. Bissell of Chicago, who is a baseball 'fiend,' dreamed he was playing ball, and the cheers were for the Cottage City nine, in which he is deeply interested. The groans and death-like yells were occasioned, he dreamed, by the umpire hitting him on the head with a bat, which caused him to cry for help."

"Then another cry was heard proceeding from No. 23. A lady, anxious to know all that was going on, put her head out through the transom. The window fell on her neck and held her head fast. The watchman released the young woman, and peace was again restored."

The Naumkeag remained a popular summer hotel through the 1930s.

1894: A *Boston Globe* reporter headed to Gay Head noted, "A peculiarity of the Vineyard roads is the width of the track, which is six inches broader than those used on the mainland; if any "off-Islander" — so called by the natives—brings his fashionable cart he will find himself with one wheel in the rut and the other bowling along on the summit of the space between."

PROFESSOR GOUGH

Professor Gough—presumably the African-American man on the far right—was the son of a former slave from Baltimore and a Vineyard-born mother of Dominican descent. Gough, who also sometimes spelled his surname "Goff," was one of the Island's first linemen,

Wheelmen pose in front of a turn-of-the-century Oak Bluffs bike shop, where the Martha's Vineyard Savings Bank stands today. The signs read "Repairing & Vulcanizing, Renting and Riding Instruction" and "Prof. Chas. F. Gough, Instructor In Our Improved 'Belt Method' Bicycle Riding." (A prominently posted flyer reads something about—a prohibition against?—"Biking through Arcade.")

stringing wires from pole to pole during the off-season. He had an interracial marriage, highly unusual for the time; his white wife Flora was an English immigrant.

Bicycling on the Vineyard reached a height of popularity in the 1890s. A *New York Herald* columnist reported in 1893, "Circling cyclists have crowded Cottage City concrete until the carriages or freight conveyance have been nearly forced to the beach sand."

GEORGE FRED

Captain George Fred Tilton of Chilmark, like his brother Zeb, is a Vineyarder of such legend that it's not even necessary to use his last name. Zeb may be better known now, but George Fred was a full-blown New England celebrity in his day. He was a rough, drunk, salty old whaler who had spent years sailing in the Pacific Arctic. Described as "a real man" and "quite a wag," a good impersonator who "could tell stories by the hour," Tilton once won a fistfight with heavyweight boxing champ Joe Choynski in a San Francisco barroom.

George Fred earned his initial fame during the winter of 1897–98, when he left on foot from the northern tip of Alaska on a two-thousand-mile adventure to find help for some three hundred whalers trapped in the ice and running out of food. He had been third mate of the steam whaler *Belvedere* of San Francisco when it became trapped in the ice with three others off Point Barrow. Another eight whalers were similarly trapped in a widely separated arc along the Alaskan coast, including the schooner *Rosario* under the command of Capt. Edwin Coffin of Edgartown. It was later named "the ice catch of 1898."

While fellow Belvedere officer and Chilmark native Stephen F. Cottle stayed behind with their vessel and crew, George Fred left for California on foot, walking, sledding, and hitching his way back to San Francisco to get help. Tilton traveled some two thousand miles in five months and twenty-two days, and ultimately made it to California, but news of the disaster had reached home months earlier, and a rescue expedition was already in progress.

In his final years, George Fred became the caretaker of the famous whaler *Charles W. Morgan*. In 1928, he wrote an autobiography, "Cap'n George Fred Himself," still found on many Island bookshelves.

DETOUR

In the early morning hours of November 27, 1898, one of New England's deadliest storms struck the Island with little warning. Known both as the Gale of 1898 and the Portland Gale, it was a blizzard of hurricane intensity. One-hundred-mile-per-hour winds buffeted Vineyard Haven with blinding snow and deadly wind chill in the predawn hours.

The British schooner *Newburgh*, returning from Staten Island to its homeport in Nova Scotia, was one of nearly one hundred coasting vessels that sought shelter in Vineyard Haven's harbor that night. But there was no shelter from this monstrous storm. The five-hundred-ton schooner (nearly the mass of a modern Steamship Authority freight boat) parted both anchor chains and crashed into the upper portion of Union Wharf. Over the next few hours, the heavy seas and high winds drove it steadily through the wharf, splintering it apart.

The *Newburgh* was one of the lucky ones: It suffered relatively little damage. Some forty other vessels were sunk or wrecked in the harbor that night, and one schooner, loaded with lime, burned to its waterline. Many lives were lost, and half-frozen survivors were carried to the Marine Hospital for medical care. The *Bethel* provided food and clothing for more than one hundred shipwrecked sailors in the days that followed.

For five months the 136-foot *Newburgh* was firmly stuck here, making the town's principal wharf impassable until necessity spawned an

The Vineyard Haven Wharf was temporarily rebuilt around the bow of the stuck schooner New-burgh *after the Gale of 1898. The* Bethel *is visible on the right.*

inventive solution: an adapted wharf with a sharp detour in the middle to direct traffic neatly around the ship's bow. When spring arrived a tugboat was brought to free the stranded schooner, and by the beginning of May the *Newburgh* was finally floated and towed to New York, leaving an unusual-shaped wharf behind. The vast amount of sand stirred up by the tug's propeller created a temporary beach that reached nearly to the end of the wharf.

FRED JAMES

Charles "Fred" James (1868–1924) was a familiar figure on Circuit Avenue at the turn of the twentieth century. The son of a blind farmer from Indian Hill, he was among the last of the "Christiantown Tribe" of Wampanoag. He was a teamster, the proprietor of a Cottage City livery stable, and ran freight with an enormous horse-drawn wagon for Chadwick's Express.

A fierce gale struck New England on a Saturday night in late November 1898, sinking or driving ashore more than thirty vessels in Vineyard Haven Harbor alone with hurricane-force winds. The schooner *Island City* was bound for Cohasset with a cargo of coal, but turned and ran for Vineyard Haven Harbor when the storm struck. It never made it. As the *New York Tribune* wrote, "She was discovered Sunday morning off Cottage City ashore, the seas making a clean breach over her. Captain Nelson and his crew of two men were in the rigging. The vessel was sighted by residents of the Island, but they were powerless to render aid. No surfboard or life-saving apparatus were available, and the nearest life-saving station was at Gay Head, twenty miles away. All wires were down, and it was impossible to communicate with the station. All the forenoon the men clung to the rigging."

In that driving snowstorm—later known as the Portland Gale—Fred James and Manuel Chaves attempted to rescue the three men from their wrecked schooner, situated just off shore between the steamer

"Fred" James (1868–1924), left, and friend share drinks on the Tivoli platform in Oak Bluffs.

wharf and Highland Wharf. Their heroic efforts ultimately failed, and they nearly lost their own lives in the attempt. The *Tribune* continued, "During the afternoon, one man was seen to drop overboard, evidently having become utterly exhausted. Soon after, the helpless watchers on the beach saw a second man relax his hold in the rigging and fall to the deck. He was quickly washed overboard. The third man remained in the rigging, apparently limp and unconscious, if not dead. He was lashed in the crosstrees, and undoubtedly perished." Two bodies were recovered the next day, and three days later the third sailor's remains washed ashore. Captain Nelson's two crewmen, whose names were never learned, became the first two interments at the new sailor's burying ground off Edgartown Road, after a well-attended funeral service.

PROFESSOR MILLER'S MILL

Professor Leslie Miller loved the tranquility of Martha's Vineyard, but as a lifelong city dweller he dearly missed one thing: running water.

Miller began his career as a portrait painter. Among the very first to attend a new public art school in Boston known today as MassArt, Miller became a highly respected lecturer and author on art education. He came to the Island in the 1870s to teach at the Martha's Vineyard Summer Institute at Cottage City, and returned every summer with his family for vacation.

Miller's career boomed. He became the first principal of a new art school in Philadelphia known today as the University of the Arts, a position he held for forty years. He supervised the layout of the Philadelphia park system, and helped design the Philadelphia Museum of Art. The *Boston Globe* called him "one of the most distinguished educators on the field of art in America." He is said to have earned the first degree of doctor of fine arts ever given in this country.

In 1889, Professor Miller bought their summer rental, a colonial farmhouse in Eastville that had belonged to Captain Peter and Almira West. One of the oldest surviving houses in Oak Bluffs, its construction has been dated to the 1740s. The Millers fixed it up and named it Tannon by the Sea. But while waterworks had been built in both Vineyard

Dr. Leslie Miller's c. 1740s home and farm, Eastville

Haven and Oak Bluffs by this time, water pipes did not yet extend anywhere near this Eastville neighborhood off County Road.

Enlisting the help of his son Arthur, a young chemical engineer, Professor Miller designed a windmill to draw water up from their well to a standpipe, and a hydraulic system to pipe the water to faucets in their home. They hired the local construction firm of Manter & Johnson to build a mill in the summer of 1897, but it blew down in a storm three months later. The following year, a second mill was erected—pictured here—and painted red. Young Arthur was the photographer of these images as well as the mill's engineer. He became a photographic emulsion chemist.

Dr. Miller retired year-round to his Oak Bluffs home in 1920. "I wouldn't live anywhere else," he told the *Boston Globe* in 1927. "I haven't been off the Island in four years."

While the 270-year-old home still stands at its original location off County Road, the windmill does not. When Oak Bluffs town water came to County Road in 1914, the windmill was dismantled. For years its base was used as a toolshed, but it was eventually demolished. A modern road called James Place covers the site today.

THE EDGARTOWN CORNET BAND

The Edgartown Cornet Band, under the direction of bandleader Richard G. Shute, played during the summer months in the late 1890s.

Chappaquiddick ferryman Charles Osborn is front and center, playing the bass drum. The tall mustachioed man playing the alto horn on the far right is Edgartown boatbuilder Rodolphus Morgan. In the second row, the second and third men from the left, just behind Osborn, are Channing Nevin and his father Bill Nevin. Bill was a lawyer who had moved to the Vineyard from Philadelphia; his son Channing would later become a popular Edgartown physician.

In the third row, second from the left and playing a cornet, is young John Wesley Mayhew. Mayhew's parents had both died by the time he was four years old, and he was adopted by his uncle Beriah Hillman. He would go on to play football for Brown University (and be named an All-American in 1906), and after a brief stint as head football coach at Louisiana State University, Mayhew would spend much of his career in China, Vietnam, and the Philippines, working for Standard Oil.

Bandleader Richard Shute—seen in the back row just behind Mayhew, with his cornet—was an Edgartown jeweler and dry goods merchant, but is best remembered as an Island photographer whose

The Edgartown Cornet Band poses on the steps of the Edgartown Town Hall about 1900.

stereoviews of the Vineyard can still be found on eBay. Shute served as a musician in the Civil War, and later played with the Vineyard Haven town band.

A poster for "Lucier's Consolidated Minstrels" is seen at the right. This group, which was billed as a "Russian Uniformed Military Band," was led by blind cornet soloist and composer Joseph Lucier. The group toured New England with an extensive entourage including blackface comics, acrobatic tumblers, clog dancers, "hoop rollers," "baton manipulators," a "bag puncher," Marguerite Lucier's "Serpentine and Spanish Dances," a slack wire performance, and a contortionist "frogman."

PART IV

TURN OF THE
CENTURY TALES

ARVAGASUGIAQPALAUQTUT KINGUVAANGINNIK QAUJINASUNGNIQ

Consumer DNA tests have become an important new tool for historians. Companies like 23andMe and AncestryDNA (which recently announced their five millionth customer) can indisputably confirm relationships as distant as fourth and fifth cousins and solve centuries-old mysteries with just a small tube of saliva.

In the 1860s, US whalers began to turn their attention to the far north, chasing bowheads in the Arctic. Many went west to the Alaskan coast, but a smaller number of New England whalers went due north instead, passing through Hudson Strait and into Hudson Bay.

Dozens of Vineyard men—poorly paid and some even shanghaied by thuggish New Bedford "crimps"—wintered over in Hudson Bay during the latter half of the nineteenth century. Many were Wampanoag, African-American, or both, like George Bolton, William Johnson, William Morton, Judson James, and G. S. Johnson. A few, like John Randall of Vineyard Haven, never made it home. (Randall was lost in the ice with a boat's crew in Hudson Bay in 1874.)

The whalers were welcomed by the Aivilingmiut people of Kivalliq and other nomadic Inuit of what is today the Canadian territory of

George Cleveland of Vineyard Haven and Nunavut—the magnificent and eccentric Sakkuaqtirungniq the Harpooner, a northern legend.

Nunavut. During long and dark Arctic winters, as they awaited a head start on the spring whaling season, relationships formed between the whalers and the local people—relationships still being untangled today. Hiram Hammett of Chilmark, of the ship *A. Houghton* (1876), was rumored to have fathered at least one Inuit child, for instance, although the child's identity has not yet been learned.

George Cleveland of Vineyard Haven (1871–1925) is certainly the most notable example. Cleveland, who was shanghaied twice and ultimately abandoned by his New Bedford employers in the unforgiving Arctic wilderness, is suspected to have fathered at least fifteen children with at least nine or ten Inuit women. Cleveland is mostly forgotten on the Vineyard, but he is very well remembered in the north, where he is known as "Sakkuaqtirungniq" ("The Harpooner"). Some idolize him; others despise him. Babies today are named after him. His larger-than-life tales can be found in numerous books and articles about the eastern

Arctic, and his character even appears in a 2006 movie, *The Journals of Knud Rasmussen*.

In just over a century, Cleveland's offspring have multiplied exponentially. It would be fair to estimate that this twentieth-century man—who shopped at Cronig's, drove in a car, and listened to the radio—has well over one thousand living descendants today, a significant fraction of the modern population of Nunavut. His Inuit offspring includes professors, musicians, web designers, ministers, journalists, civil servants, radio hosts, artists, poets, interpreters, and social workers, across the Canadian Arctic. Most of them, it seems, are on Facebook. And some of them have begun to match DNA with their Vineyard cousins.

Susan Sammurtok of Iqaluit, granddaughter of Cleveland's Inuit daughter Siksik, writes: "His genes were very strong amongst the Inuit. There are some who resemble him a lot, look so much like him."

Sarah Nangmalik of Iqaluit, granddaughter of Cleveland's Inuit daughter Ipiksaut, writes: "Several in my family are named 'Sakkuak-tirungniq' after Capt. George Cleveland. There are tons and tons of his family up here. Many of us know each other."

Judy Swan of Huntington Beach, California, is the granddaughter of florist Lewellyn Cleveland of Vineyard Haven, one of the two Vineyard-born children George left behind on the Island. She writes: "Stories of him have been passed down the family. When George visited his family on the Vineyard in 1923, he was an unusual person to the two grandchildren old enough to remember him. He told outrageous stories, and mealtime was an anomaly to them as George ate with a knife. However he was viewed, George Cleveland was truly a legend."

Arvagasugiaqpalauqtut Kinguvaanginnik Qaujinasungniq ("Whalers DNA Project" in Inuktitut) is dedicated to identifying Martha's

Vineyard whalers who have living Inuit descendants in Nunavut and the Hudson Bay area, and to reunite distant cousins from north and south.

Anyone related to a Vineyard whaler who wintered in Hudson Bay may want to get his or her DNA tested!

THE STEAMER
MARTHA'S VINEYARD

The sidewheel steamer *Martha's Vineyard* was one of the four original steamships owned by the enterprise now known as the Steamship Authority. Built in 1871 in Brooklyn, it was some 185 feet long (about forty-five feet shorter than the modern vessel of this name), with a separate ladies' saloon, and stewards to take care of passenger comforts.

In the early morning of June 6, 1903, under the command of Captain Claghorn, the *Martha's Vineyard* set out on its scheduled run from Vineyard Haven to Woods Hole in a thick fog, carrying a large number of passengers, the mail, and a heavy load of freight. With little warning, it collided with a Gloucester mackerel seiner, *Senator Saulsbury*, anchored just outside the harbor.

As the *New York Times* reported, "The vessels struck with great force. The steamer's bow struck the schooner forward, the bowsprit of the fisherman raking the steamboat, carrying away both the upper and the lower decks back to the paddlebox. The fore rigging of the vessel became entangled in the wreckage and was carried away. Russell Hancock of Chilmark, a passenger on the steamboat, was badly injured, and several other passengers, unable to escape the sweep of the schooner bowsprit, were knocked insensible." Hancock was a sixty-two-year-old

The steamer Martha's Vineyard

Chilmark native and former whaler who had long since taken up the gentler pursuits of farming, Sunday school teaching, and carving duck decoys. He was traveling that morning with his wife, Susan.

The damage was all above the waterline, so the *Martha's Vineyard* managed to limp into Woods Hole an hour later. The unconscious passengers had revived with only minor injuries, but Hancock was rushed to a doctor. His wounds, though bloody, ultimately proved not to be life threatening.

THE CIGAR SMOKING MACHINE

In 1904, Edgartown inventor Elmer Bliss was issued patent 768,892 for a life-size automaton designed to advertise tobacco products. It smoked real cigars by alternately drawing in and distending lifelike human cheeks with a hidden battery-powered pump.

Said to be a lookalike of President Harrison, Bliss founded the Regal Shoe Company, a major ladies' shoe manufacturer based in Boston with four massive factories and a chain of international shoe stores. Grandson of Edgartown whaling captain Jared Fisher, Bliss summered in his childhood home on the Island, from which he filed many of his patents throughout the early 1900s—mostly for sizing feet, shoes, and gloves, but also for chairs, awnings, and advertising contraptions like this one.

Bliss caused a stir in 1900 when he drove through town in a steam-powered "locomobile," which he had brought down from Boston, thought to be the first automobile on the Island. With his shoe fortunes, Bliss purchased Osborne Wharf, revived the Edgartown Yacht Club, funded and built the clubhouse, and served as its commodore.

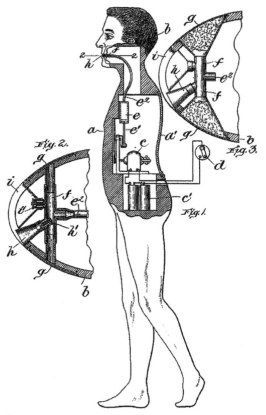

Patent No. 768,892. *"Advertising device . . . intended to advertise cigars, cigarettes, and the like by the use of a human model constructed and arranged to smoke the cigars automatically."*

1904: A severe December blizzard struck the island, dumping twenty inches of snow. "Vineyard Haven a Scene of Havoc," wrote the *New York Evening Post*. Of the forty or so vessels in harbor, "hardly one escaped injury." Five collisions were reported, and a number of schooners were driven ashore in Vineyard Haven Harbor. A three-masted British schooner full of lumber went ashore in Cottage City, and another three-master went aground near Squibnocket.

FANCY POULTRY

When new millionaire William Barry Owen retired from the gramophone business in London and headed back to his native Vineyard Haven in 1904, he packed some unusual souvenirs for his long voyage home: an entire flock of Buff Orpingtons, a variety of "fancy" English chickens raised for neither meat nor eggs, but for show. Upon winning a fistful of awards at the Poultry, Pigeon, and Pet Stock exhibition at Madison Square Garden in 1905, Owen bought fifteen more prize birds from a fellow exhibitor for a jaw-dropping $1,550. Included in the purchase was a single five-hundred-dollar bird that was to become the "Owen Farms Champion," genesis of a legendary line of Martha's Vineyard thoroughbred fowl.

Owen next caused what the *American Poultry Journal* described as "a furor in the poultry world." He purchased three vast Island properties: Red Farm, a seventy-acre tract in Lambert's Cove; and two adjacent lots known collectively as Tashmoo Farms, consisting of 110 acres of oak trees and meadow sprawling from Oak Grove Cemetery to the shores of Lake Tashmoo, on both sides of what is now West Spring Street. He then recruited two of the foremost experts in the country on the breeding and mating of exhibition poultry—Maurice Delano and Frank Davey—together with a team of local farm workers and office staff. In just a few months, Owen had created the largest fancy poultry farm in the world.

Using incubators built for three thousand eggs, eight thousand chicks were raised each year at Owen Farms, and five thousand adult birds populated seventy-five chicken houses, eight 117-foot-long breeding houses, and acres of pens and runs. They distributed fifty thousand copies of their illustrated circular, and five thousand copies of their thick catalog, filling orders of hatching eggs from as far away as South Africa, South America, Australia, and New Zealand. Owen Farms took twenty-seven first prizes out of forty-eight at the Madison Square Garden show in 1911; by 1918 they had amassed 417 blue ribbons from the Garden show alone. In 1913, Owen retired and Delano bought the business. American Poultry magazine called it "the greatest poultry establishment in the world."

Delano ultimately went bankrupt in 1929, and the Owen Farm properties were broken up and sold. Senator William Butler bought Red Farm, annexing it to his vast estate known as Mohu, and Tashmoo Farms was ultimately subdivided into dozens of house lots. Delano left the Island and found work as an advertiser and cattle feed salesman, but he continued serving as a highly respected fancy poultry show judge until his death in 1960.

In 1906, the *Boston Globe* reported, "After much agitation over changing the name of this town from Cottage City back to its original one, Oak Bluffs, the originators of the idea have at last made a dramatic move in the form of petitions which are being circulated about town. The project is gaining in favor daily and the petitions have been signed by a large number of taxpayers, particularly among the summer residents." A year later, the *Globe* reported the outcome: "Marked enthusiasm greeted the news that Cottage City was hereafter to be known as 'Oak Bluffs.' Bells were rung, salutes fired, and flags and bunting displayed."

GIFFORD'S BOATYARD

Ship's carpenter and boatbuilder Charles Gifford was born on Penikese Island—then known as Pune Island, and still technically part of Chilmark—where the Gifford family lived and tended sheep. Moving to Holmes Hole after the end of the Civil War, he lived with his wife Betsy in their home on Water Street (near Five Corners,

Shipwright Charles Gifford (1833–1910) lays the keel of a new vessel at his boatyard shop in Vineyard Haven.

demolished in 2015), and ran a boat shop near the marine railway on Beach Road.

In his 1907 memoir *The History of Cedar Neck*, author Charles Hine wrote fondly of his memories of Gifford and his shop:

> The harbor waves rippled on the beach at his door, and always were there boats in the making or repairing. One day there wandered into his shop a couple of young men who found the boatbuilder down on his back doing a bit of caulking. Now Mr. Gifford was possessed of a beard that was of some length, and the strange young visitors immediately became fascinated with the thought that next time he would surely caulk his whiskers into the seam, and soon they were laying bets, and it is said they stayed a goodly part of the day in the firm conviction that it must happen soon, but Mr. Gifford still wears his whiskers, for he had been there many a time before.

Gifford's shop eventually became part of what is today the Martha's Vineyard Shipyard.

In 1908, the Massachusetts Supreme Court ruled that farmer Henry Davis was not entitled to the establishment of a school on Nomans. Davis had demanded that the town of Chilmark provide a school for his five children, aged four, twelve, seventeen, nineteen, and twenty-four, the only children on that island. The court denied his claim, stating "He cannot expect the town to furnish and maintain a school for his sole benefit."

By 1914, the Davis clan had moved to West Tisbury, and another family with three young children had taken up residence. *The Indianapolis News* described, "There are three or four old fishing shanties on the island, the largest and most substantial dwelling being the home of the Swenson family. . . . The village of Fishville, which many years ago had a considerable population during the fishing season, has gradually crumbled away until of the twenty-odd fishing shacks which comprise this little settlement, all but three or four have collapsed from age or been burned. The island is a part of the town of Chilmark."

THE PIRATES OF LAKE TASHMOO

Performed over three August days, *The Pageant of Lake Tashmoo* was billed as "A Historical Drama of the Discovery, Settlement and Incidents of the Revolutionary War, at the Island of Martha's Vineyard, and Particularly at the Village of Vineyard Haven." In the photo, Brown, a Vineyard Haven lawyer and amateur playwright, assumes the role of early-seventeenth-century "pirate captain" Thomas Hunt in Act I, Scene III: "The Incursion of Captain Hunt."

The *Christian Science Monitor* reported, "Most of the 190 persons taking part were lineal descendants of characters whose parts they were taking." Many of the props were authentic relics, like a powder horn from the French and Indian War, a two-hundred-year-old ceremonial Native American pipe, a renowned New Bedford whaleboat, and costumes that were family heirlooms. Few, if any, of the cast were Wampanoag, evident from the many uncomfortable photos taken at the pageant depicting nontribal actors in redface and feathers. On the pageant's opening day, the *New York Sun* noted, "the stores were closed and the town assumed all the aspect of a gala day."

Much of Act I told the true story of Epenow (played by Roy Mathews, not pictured), who made fools of his English captors. Kidnapped from the Island in 1611, Epenow was brought to Lon-

From left, Marcus Smith, John B. Luce, Charles Brown, Ben Norton, Frank Golart, and Frank Lynch ham it up as a pirate crew in 1913's The Pageant of Lake Tashmoo.

don as a "wonder" of the New World (and as the likely model of the "strange Indian" in *Henry VIII*, he is the only Vineyarder to appear in Shakespeare's works). Convincing his captors that a rich gold mine awaited them on Martha's Vineyard, Epenow returned to the Island as their guide, only to escape in a hail of arrows launched by his Vineyard friends. The pageant's script confuses Capt. Thomas Hunt (who enslaved natives along the Massachusetts coast, most notably Tiasquantum, or "Squanto") for his contemporary, Capt. Edward Harlow, believed to be Epenow's actual captor.

Amateur actors all, Smith was a blacksmith, Luce an electrical contractor, Brown an attorney, Norton a stonemason, Golart a telephone lineman, and Lynch a boatman.

TISBURY HIGH BASKETBALL, 1913

Meet Jed, Phinn, Chick, Frog, Bill and Dolf—the Tisbury High School basketball team of 1913–14.

Jesse J. "Jed" Oliver (1897–1957) played "forward guard." An Azorean native, Oliver later became a fisherman and ran a filling station in Vineyard Haven.

Theodore C. "Phinn" Howes (1896–1968) played forward and also served as manager of the team. The son of a Vineyard Haven clothing merchant, Ted Howes later became a bank clerk and insurance agent.

George Philip "Chicken" Baptiste (1895–1966) played center. He later became an automobile mechanic at Dukes County Garage on Five Corners.

Donald S. "Frog" Swift (1898–1943) played "sub." The son of a Vineyard Haven grocer, Swift later became a civil engineer and realtor.

William E. "Bill" Carroll (1898–1983) played guard. A chauffeur, truck driver, and steamship agent, he later founded the moving company today known as "Carroll's."

Bill's older brother Frank "Dolf" Carroll (1896–1923) played "forward guard" and also served as captain of the team. Frank died of a heart condition at the age of twenty-seven.

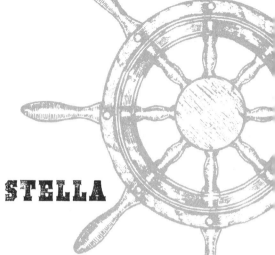

STELLA

S tella Abiah Ryan was born in 1885 in the town once known as Gay
Head, the daughter of Charles Ryan and Rachel Diamond of Lob-
sterville. Her father, a white man from Long Island, was a lobsterman.
Her mother, a Gay Head–born Wampanoag woman, ran a summer
boarding house out of their family homestead known as "the House at
Nestle Nook." Charles would take their well-to-do summer guests in
his oxcart to the beach for clambakes.

During an era when higher educational opportunities for young
women and men of color were very limited, the proceeds from Nestle
Nook allowed Stella's sister Eva to be sent to music school, her brother
Bill to Carlisle Indian School for vocational training in plumbing, and
her brother Grover to art school. Stella boarded temporarily at the
home of the assistant drawbridge tender in New Bedford to earn her
diploma at New Bedford High School in 1910, at the age of twenty-
five.

Stella's pastor at the Gay Head Baptist Church, where her mom
served as both trustee and clerk, had for the previous five years been the
Rev. Clarence Whitman of Minnesota, who had graduated from the
Newton Theological Institution and then spent two years as a missionary in the Belgian Congo before coming to Gay Head. Whitman had
brought with him a large quantity of photographs and artifacts he had
collected in the Congo, which he undoubtedly shared with his Vineyard

Taking Aquinnah summer visitors to the beach via oxcart was once a lucrative summer trade.

parishioners, including Stella and her family. In 1910, Whitman left the church in Gay Head to become a missionary in the town of Donga, Nigeria, on the border of Cameroon. Inspired by him, Stella decided to continue her education at her pastor's alma mater, the Newton Theological Institution in Boston (today known as Gordon College).

All of Stella's siblings settled permanently on the Vineyard. Two of them, Grover and Eva, would spend their lives at Nestle Nook. Grover was a Vineyard house painter who also dabbled in fine arts, while Bill became an up-Island plumber. But when Stella finished her studies, she decided instead to teach in Nigeria, where her former pastor continued to work.

Stella left the United States in July 1913 on the White Star liner *Celtic*, and arrived in Donga, Nigeria, two months later. She taught at the mission school in Donga for sixteen months under the auspices of the Sudan United Mission, learning the Hausa language and translating textbooks and the Bible. They discovered that converting the locals to Christianity was an uphill battle; as Whitman would report in 1915,

"For every one convert to Christ's teaching there have been forty or fifty to Mohammedanism." To better blend in, Stella and Whitman adopted Islamic dress. They studied the local textile industry and dyeing methods, and collected fabrics, furniture, and other items to bring back for educational use in American schools, together with many photographs.

After a winter back home, Stella departed again for Donga in January 1917. But her love of Nigeria might not have been entirely responsible for drawing her back. According to her niece and namesake, Stella Hopkins of Aquinnah, by the time of her second stint in Nigeria, Stella Ryan "was to be married to an English trader." A railroad had recently been built from the coast past Donga, and with it came British business. Both John Holt & Company of Liverpool and the Niger Company Ltd. of London had local representatives in Donga, purchasing palm oil, textiles, and goatskin for European wholesale.

The wedding never took place. Stella died November 22, 1918, from a fever, perhaps malaria, and is buried in Donga. The church where she worked, now the Christian Reformed Church of Nigeria, continues to remember Stella Ryan of Gay Head and Reverend Whitman on their website. On the Island, a brass plaque dedicated to Stella can be found at the Gay Head Community Baptist Church.

SEVENTH GRADE

M eet Tisbury School's seventh grade class of 1914–15 in the old schoolhouse on Center Street. Front row: Catherine Conroy, Stan Lair, James Andrews, Rebecca Carey, _____. Second row: Evelyn Norton, Alice Stevenson, Clara Rogers, Emma Luce, Onslow Robinson. Third row: Mary Andrews, Kathleen McDonough, Dorothy Cleveland, Helen Howland, Camillo Mello. Back row: Marjorie Isaacs, Ellery Norton, Alfreda West, Howard Mathews, and Ruth Andrews. Miss Smith, teacher.

1914: Six hundred tons of shells from Chesapeake Bay were shipped to Vineyard Haven and crushed for the road to West Chop. [*Vineyard Gazette*]

WALTER & DOROTHY

Walter Jenney, a New Bedford blacksmith's son, came to the Vineyard just after the turn of the twentieth century, and clerked for the Vineyard Haven grocery of Bodfish & Call. He soon bought a home in West Tisbury with his wife Rebecca ("Reba") and their only child Dorothy. He was a meatcutter by trade.

By the First World War, Walter had begun work with the S. M. Mayhew Company (precursor to Alley's). Renting a house on Middle Road, he became the manager of the Chilmark Store (under S. M. Mayhew ownership), and served as Chilmark's assistant postmaster as well.

Eventually, Walter went back to work for his first employer, which had merged to become the conglomerate grocery of Smith Bodfish & Swift. As S.B.S.'s up-Island "general provisions salesman," Walter delivered groceries to the west half of the Island, sometimes accompanied by Reba.

A rambunctious "tomboy," Dorothy was "definitely the apple of his eye" according to her daughter Carol (Jenney) Christensen of West Tisbury. Dorothy would later become a teacher—she taught junior high school English and ancient history in Edgartown—and later moved to Hopkinton. Dorothy died in 2008, at the age of one hundred.

Walter Jenney of West Tisbury poses with his daughter Dorothy, before 1915.

1915: A baseball game pitted members of the Fifth Regiment of the Massachusetts Volunteer Militia against a local Oak Bluffs team. "The soldiers marched into the game in companies," reported the *Boston Globe*. Oak Bluffs won, four to one, but the day became even more exciting when

Capt. Jack Caldwell's mule brigade invaded Waban Park during the ball game in an "impromptu Wild West exhibition." "The animal's tails were tied with red and yellow ribbons [and] their bridles decked with bright paper plumes." A mule race was organized with twenty participants, and although his mule balked in the home stretch, private J. W. Parmenter of M Company was first under the wire, winning first place. A few days earlier in Katama, the Fifth Regiment's machine gun company had practiced firing thousands of rounds at some twenty-five hundred balloons, representing an enemy force entrenched behind the sand dunes.

WELCOME AND THE APE

Welcome Tilton of Chilmark (1856–1949) was a whaleman, trap fisherman, lobsterman, cod fisherman, coaster, fishmonger, and later in life, door-to-door vanilla salesman. He came from a family of colorful characters—his brothers George Fred (who walked home from the Arctic) and Zeb (the cross-eyed schooner captain) perhaps the most famous among them. But Welcome was the first to see the Chilmark ape.

In late August 1915, Welcome was working in the woods when he spotted a large animal. At first he thought it was a young black bear, unseen on Martha's Vineyard for at least three hundred years. "It was heavy-limbed and black. Stood I should judge about three feet in height. The head was big and rounded, his teeth were white and prominent," he would tell a *Boston Globe* reporter. Then the animal turned on him; "It made for me." Welcome fled to his house, fetched a gun and his brothers, but when he returned the animal had vanished.

Retired "country gentleman" George Eustis of Hollyholm Farm in Chilmark spotted it next. In the middle of the night, he heard a commotion in his henhouse, and saw a dark form about three feet tall scampering across his field on all fours. He then found his turkey nest robbed of eggs, and a trail of sucked eggs leading into the woods. The next morning he found a footprint, the size of a child's.

Not long ago the Vineyard was home to both red and gray foxes, mink, red squirrel, muskrat, otter, and possibly black bear. Early

European explorers also reported beaver, bobcat, and martens on the Vineyard, as well as an extra-large, stripeless variety of native skunk. Going much further back in time, fossils of wild horses, camels, rhinoceri, and even gomphotheres (close cousins of mastodons and elephants) have been unearthed at Aquinnah. But nobody had ever reported a wild simian on Martha's Vineyard before.

That's not to say the Vineyard hadn't had any primate pets. Rural mail carrier Fred Luce recalled a sailor at the Marine Hospital in Vineyard Haven who had a pet ape. "This animal was so obnoxious that the authorities killed him and his body was cremated in the hospital furnace," he reported.

The colorful Putnam family also kept monkeys and chimpanzees at their home at Valleydale Farm, off North Road (now part of Spring Point). Dr. Charles Putnam, a wealthy ear, nose, and throat surgeon from Manhattan, and his wife Angelica owned a sprawling farm where they raised a large family of children and kept monkeys as pets. (Their son Patrick would later become a famously eccentric anthropologist who lived in the Belgian Congo with the Mbuti Pygmies, and would occasionally bring home chimps to live in their Chilmark farm and later to his sister's home in Vineyard Haven. Patrick also gave his parents an alligator, which lived in their New York apartment until it escaped.) But in 1915, the Putnam family's pet monkeys were safe and secure in their cage. Mrs. Putnam begged the public not to kill the creature should it be found. She offered to help capture it and felt confident that they could succeed.

Forrest Bosworth saw it next in broad daylight on North Road. He reported it as "big as a man, but rather short" with big white teeth, hairy body, and long tail. It scampered away into a swamp, frightened by Bosworth's dog. Bosworth and Ernest Cardoze spent the next day armed with guns hunting the animal, but found nothing.

The *Boston Post* took the story less seriously than the *Globe*, and printed a long, snarky, tongue-in-cheek report. "There is an ape running amuck down in the vicinity of the Chilmark jungle," reported the *Post*; "it measures anywhere from one foot to 11 feet in height. It steals eggs, kills hens, and scares men, women, and children. . . . If stories keep going the rounds about the ape a few more days, a herd of elephants will be running amuck down off Gay Head."

But the *Post* was accurate in its assessment of the hysteria that had enveloped the Vineyard—"a regular Edgar Allan Poe 'Rue Morgue' gorilla mystery." Ape stories grew "thick and fast." Eustis had to put a sign up to keep curious trespassers away. Eleven-year-old Martha Murray saw a figure off North Road, and declared, "It wasn't a man." The animal was seen the same night in Squibnocket and in Edgartown. ("If these stories are true, I'll have to lay for Mr. Ape and arrest him for over-speeding" the *Post* reportedly quoted Chief Osgood Mayhew of the Oak Bluffs Police.) Blacksmith "Tut" Chase of North Tisbury deduced that it must be an orangutan. The leading theory was that the animal dropped or was thrown from a passing ship, and swam ashore. "Remarkable stories were rife," concluded the *Globe*.

Unless a reader has further information, the ape was never seen again. But keep an eye on your henhouse.

1915: Isabella De Grasse, twenty-five, of Oak Bluffs was arrested for attempting to kill her husband, Manuel. She allegedly put an arsenic-based rat poison in her husband's cup of tea over a period of twenty-four days. Manuel made a living digging clams and catching fish, and Isabella sold his fish, house to house, "pulling it about in a rude little cart made of a large box set on a pair of small wheels," according to the *Boston Globe*, and accompanied by her three-year-old daughter. He became seriously ill, but recovered.

THE ICE YACHTS

Before the 1938 hurricane (and the subsequent dredging of a wide, permanent channel into Vineyard Sound), Tashmoo was mostly freshwater and prone to freezing over mid-winter with a layer of ice more than six inches thick. A popular spot for ice-skating, Tashmoo was also home to a more unusual sport: iceboating.

As the *Boston Globe* wrote in 1898, "There is probably no place this side of the Hudson where there is as much interest taken in ice yachting as on the Island of Martha's Vineyard." That winter, eleven ice boats regularly raced each other, including *Dude* (Arthur C. Francis) and *Diabo* (Frank C. Tripp), considered the fastest of the fleet that year; *Tricksey* (Frank and George Golart); *Blue Bird* (Carlton Lair); *Fanny* (Leroy Lair); *Foranaft* (Dr. Edward Roth); *Game Cock* (Charles Brown) and *Skip Jack* (John Randolph). *Dude* and *Tricksey* suffered a serious collision in 1897, breaking the leg of *Dude*'s owner.

A new generation of iceboaters ventured out in the 1920s and early 1930s, including Dr. Orland S. Mayhew, William E. Dugan, Frank Bodfish, Frank Swift, Charles "Duffy" Vincent, Morton Vincent, John "Crocker" Andrews, Benjamin C. Crowell, Rodney Cleveland, and Capt. Hartson Bodfish. Vineyard Haven resident Walter Renear (1925–2002) recalled, "[Hartson] Bodfish's and Mayhew's were big boats with large cockpits capable of holding six to eight people. I was a passenger many times in both."

John "Crocker" Andrew and Charles "Duffy" Vincent and the iceboat Miss Flapper, *about 1930 on Tashmoo.*

Today, Tashmoo is a saltwater estuary; it is very dangerous to venture out on any ice that forms.

1915: Twenty-four automobiles were seen outside the Eagleston Theatre in Vineyard Haven on a Saturday night in December, which the *Vineyard Gazette* called a "sight really worth seeing." The Eagleston Theatre (formerly the Capawock) had opened that fall, complete with a five-person private balcony. The opening feature was *The Vampire* starring Olga Petrova: admission, fifteen cents. The *Gazette* reported an "immense crowd."

TIVOLI GIRL

Come! Come! Tivoli Girl, dance the hours away; –
Come! Come! Tivoli Girl, don't you hear the music play?
If you'll be my pal in the summertime down beside the ocean blue,
When the snow flies, Tivoli Girl, I'll be dreaming of you . . .

—"TIVOLI GIRL," WILL HARDY, 1917

Will Hardy was king of the Tivoli. As bandleader and musical director of the popular dance hall in Oak Bluffs (located where the police station is today), his six-piece orchestra from Worcester was a fixture of the Oak Bluffs music scene every summer from 1915 until 1931. Hardy wrote and performed original songs like "Dear Old Martha's Vineyard" (1915), "Here Comes the 'Sankaty' with My Best Girl on Board" (1917) ("We met last summer at the old 'Pawnee,' the old 'Pawnee'; We danced together at the 'Tivoli' . . ."), and arguably his most popular song, the waltz "Tivoli Girl" (1917).

While Hardy was the public face of the Tivoli, the back of the house was run by the Tivoli's proprietor (and Hardy's boss), Ray Wells of Falmouth. Wells was Falmouth's longtime fire chief and a Teaticket insurance agent, but he spent his summers in Oak Bluffs, managing the Tivoli.

On the morning of Thursday, July 27, 1916, while passing Farm Pond, Mr. Wells stopped to investigate a "bundle" floating in about two feet of water, which had been observed by passersby for several days. It was the decomposing body of a thirty-six-year-old woman dressed only in her undergarments, wearing one shoe. Her name was written on the waistband of her underwear: Miss Henrietta McLeod of Milton. An autopsy revealed that she was missing her front upper and lower teeth—believed to have been knocked out—and that her lungs were empty of water, suggesting that drowning may not have been the cause of death. It would later be learned that she was missing a gold ring. A murder investigation began, led by State Police inspector Thomas Dexter.

Miss McLeod had last been seen on Sunday morning, July 9, wearing a black skirt and a colorful Panama hat, carrying a parasol. A Nova Scotia native, McLeod had been hired as a live-in "nurse girl" for a Swedish dentist and professor, Dr. Sverker Luttropp of Boston, providing both meals and childcare for his family. Two weeks after she was hired, the Luttropp family traveled to their summer home in Oak Bluffs, where Mrs. Luttropp's mother, Maria Silvia Bettencourt, lived. Unfortunately Miss McLeod was not a good cook, and the night before her disappearance she was fired. The following morning she packed her wicker valise and leather bag and set off for the ferry with a train ticket to Boston and three dollars, but instead of boarding the steamer, two milkmen saw her turn toward Circuit Avenue to buy something to eat at William Ripley's lunch cart. After that, the trail went cold. The *Boston Post* reported, "Officer Dexter believes that she was enticed away from the dock by some shady characters, who loiter about that section, to some lonely place and slain."

Wells's discovery was in a remote, heavily wooded section of Farm Pond, far from any houses. After an initial unsuccessful police search of the area, the authorities put slides in the motion picture houses around the Island to announce an emergency Boy Scout meeting. Thirty scouts turned out the next day to systematically search the woods, and almost immediately the boys discovered more clues near the edge of the pond:

Miss McLeod's other shoe; her skirt, hanging from a tree; a pile of leaves used as a bed and showing signs of a struggle; a second makeshift bed laid out from the contents of her valise; and a letter addressed to McLeod bearing a Boston postmark, torn into pieces too small to read.

Although her family in Milton emphatically believed that Henrietta had been murdered, the Luttropp family suggested that she had committed suicide, as she "acted in a peculiar manner" at times and seemed somewhat "dazed" on the morning she left. On the third day after Wells's discovery, the police declared the McLeod case a suicide and closed it. The *Boston Post* reported, "It is believed that while temporarily deranged she tore off her skirts and leaped into the pond." Neither the gold ring nor the contents of the letter were ever recovered.

CUTTING ICE

Ernest Pease spent his youth toiling in his father Louis's "Globe Fish Market" on Circuit Avenue, before purchasing the ice business of Osgood Mayhew in 1914. Mayhew went on to become Oak Bluffs chief of police, but Pease continued his ice operation into the 1930s. Stan Lair (1902–1987) of Vineyard Haven recalled, "It was quite a sight to see the old ice man arrive, and always had a bunch of kids trailing along behind to get the slivers of ice as he would cut a cake in half with his ice pick. Kids always followed the truck around and got the slivers."

It's 1917—less than a decade before Kelvinator began advertising electric "iceless refrigerators" in Ladies' Home Journal *and* Good Housekeeping. *Laborers cut and load ice at Ernest Pease's icehouse on Crystal Lake in Oak Bluffs. Coal barges can be seen in the harbor in the background.*

SALVAGING THE PORT HUNTER

At 1:48 a.m. on the moonless early morning of November 2, 1918, the four-thousand-ton British steamship *Port Hunter* collided with the ocean tug *Covington* while en route from Boston to New York. The tug made a massive gash in the side of the steamer, the impact knocking twenty crewmen out of their berths, injuring four. The skipper managed to ground the 380-foot freighter on the slope of nearby Hedge Fence Shoal. The crew barely had time to evacuate before the wreck sank, ultimately sliding into deeper water and breaking in two.

The steamer was filled with supplies for US soldiers fighting in France and had been scheduled to rendezvous with a convoy headed for St. Nazaire. The cargo, valued at between five and seven million dollars, contained more than two hundred tons of steel, together with motorcycles and automobiles, railroad car wheels, freight cars, machine guns, phosphorous bombs, millions of rounds of ammunition, and huge quantities of clothing, including five million pairs of shoes, one million uniforms, two hundred fifty thousand leather jackets, and ten thousand pairs of rubber boots.

Stan Lair of Vineyard Haven, a teenager at the time, recalled, "We got the word that cargo boxes were coming ashore on the north side of the Island, so a bunch of us boys headed down toward the Herring

Salvager Dave Curney (in diving suit, left) on the Nickerson *at the site of the* Port Hunter *wreck, circa 1918–19.*

Creek, about a three-mile walk through the woods. We arrived there, and sure enough, there were all sorts of things coming ashore in boxes. There were leather jerkins, there were leather vests lined with olive drab wool, long woolen underwear, there were wool socks, olive drab shirts, trousers, matching wool puttees—those were the puttees that they used to wrap around their legs. Lots of soap—boxes of soap were aboard there."

Others flocked to the scene of the wreck on fishing boats, dropping hooks into the holds to liberate even more cargo.

Lair continues: "For a time, there was 'finders keepers,' and fishermen were bringing leather jerkins into the town wharf, and selling them right off the boats for a dollar apiece. And they were bringing those things in by the hundreds. That brought all the merchants from New Bedford here, every boat that came in was loaded with them to buy up some of this stuff. I recall a drayload of rubber boots going up past my house on Centre Street, just heaped right up with new rubber boots. Then the Coast Guard made the announcement that everything must be turned in to them at the Vineyard Haven wharf. They had an armed guard there on patrol. Nobody paid any attention to it. I don't know how much stuff got turned in; I don't think it was very much. But they tried anyway."

It took nearly three months for the federal government to work out a salvaging plan, complicated by the fact the vessel was British-owned, and some of the cargo was a French consignment. In January, a dispatch was issued declaring that persons purchasing salvaged cargo without permission would be liable to prosecution. It was widely ignored.

The official salvaging contract was finally awarded to Barney Zeitz of the Mercantile Wrecking Company of New Bedford (and great-uncle and namesake of the local Vineyard sculptor). Stories were circulated that Zeitz's salvage crew was armed with rifles and would shoot any unauthorized boats that approached. But it was nearly too late—more than two million dollars worth of cargo had already disappeared. "Nearly everyone on Cape Cod was wearing Army and Navy clothing after the wreck," reported the *New York Times*.

Lair said: "Zeitz hired the sanitary laundry in Oak Bluffs, all fifty or so [employees], to launder these things. They'd been in saltwater of course. They were washed, pressed, packaged, and sold to mainland buyers. They would hang these out to dry in the yard by the laundry. There's a fence around the area, almost like a chainlink fence. In the evening, why, men on the outside of the fence would come equipped with fish lines and poles and throw the line over the fence and hook out a few leather vests and so forth. Well, they were worth three or four dollars apiece, so there was a lot of pirating going around. Also it wasn't safe to hang your vests out on the line to dry at your home along with your wash, 'cause you'd look out the next morning and the whole thing would be gone, including your family wash. There were a bunch of pirates around here in those days!"

Over the years the *Port Hunter* has attracted further salvage attempts, fueled by tales of hidden gold, jewelry, and shipments of brandy still aboard, but none has proven profitable. The wreck remains submerged today, nearly intact, less than two miles off East Chop.

A FULL BATH MORE
THAN ONCE A WEEK

In 1919, the Child Health Organization of America, in cooperation with the US Bureau of Education, formulated eight rules to a "health game" in a broad effort to promote health education in schools across the country. The health game, "A Contest in Which the Government Plays," was promoted throughout the early 1920s by the Red Cross, popular magazines, and future president Herbert Hoover, often through its mascot, "CHO-CHO the Clown." *Good Housekeeping* magazine

Students from the old Tisbury School on Center Street march with towels and soap.

wrote, "The aim is to put the play spirit into health work, making of it a game whose rules are positive rather than negative. Every child wants to play a winning game." In addition to the suggestion on these students' sign, the other rules of the game included "Sleeping long hours with windows open," "Drinking as much milk as possible, but no coffee or tea," "Drinking at least four glasses of water a day," and "Playing part of every day out of doors."

The Center Street school included Tisbury Grammar School (grades 1–8) and Tisbury High School (9–12). The high school also served, on a tuition basis, a few students from West Tisbury, Chilmark, and Gay Head. An overflow structure known as the "Portable Building" can be seen on the right, and Center Street is visible in the background. The school closed in 1929, and today the town tennis courts occupy this location.

PART V

THE 1920S

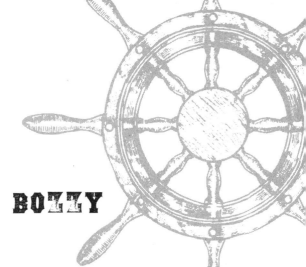

BOZZY

About 1918, Bozzy the alligator arrived in Vineyard Haven, where he would live for many years in the warm interior of the Barnacle Club under the gentle care of his custodian, George "Goody" Fisher. The alligator, about thirteen years old and perhaps two feet in length, was named for the tug *Boswell* on which he arrived from the Florida Keys. He soon took the role of the club's mascot. On warmer days, Bozzy would be found dozing in a pan full of warm water (changed by Fisher five or six times a day) in the club's downtown windows. At night, and in the winter, Bozzy would sleep behind the big base burner stove.

Fisher "simply dotes on alligators" wrote the *Vineyard Gazette* in 1921, as he demonstrated how Bozzy enjoyed being flipped over and having his stomach and throat stroked. The gator was kept company by a snapping turtle named Pete, later by two turtles, Pro and Con, and eventually by Louie Loggerhead, a "vicious snapping turtle." In the spring of 1921, he was joined by a second alligator known as "Dickey" (or sometimes "Robbie Dickie"), named for Robert L. Dickey, a nationally famous dog cartoonist who shipped it to the club from Florida as a gift. The two alligators would sun themselves together in the club's wide windows. "They love each other now," noted the *Gazette* in 1921; "If one alligator is removed to another part of the room, he croaks like a frog until his chum answers." In 1922, two additional alligators were presented to the club by summer Edgartown resident Julien Vose, piano manufacturer. The two unnamed gators, both hatchlings less than a foot long, had been sent to Vose by parcel post from California.

It's unclear what became of the alligators and turtles after Fisher's death in 1923. The gators were not fond of anyone other than Fisher. "They have a decided grudge against most of the world, and regard only their custodian with some degree of favor," wrote the *Gazette* in 1921. "[Bozzy] regards his keeper with something like affection, although he still eats his food from the tip of a hatpin, lest he mistake a kindly hand for a hunk of the raw beefsteak." A 1922 account adds, "You are almost prepared to stroke Bozzy's knobby back and say 'nice Bozzy, nice Bozzy.' But you don't. A warning hiss, not at all friendly, warns you that nice Bozzy is not about to purr. And you put your hand hastily into your pocket, instead of into his pan."

ALE AND CORPSES

At the annual town meeting in 1919, Oak Bluffs voted to go from "dry" to "wet," allowing the town to offer permits for saloons to sell liquor. (Edgartown voted to stay dry that year, according to the *Boston Globe*, "as usual.") The public mood had swung back and forth many times over the years. Cottage City had voted "wet" in 1899, but "dry" in 1900, only to vote "wet" again in 1902 and 1903. Finally, Prohibition went into effect nationwide in 1920.

In 1923, eight corpses were found floating in Vineyard Sound off the Chilmark shore, Cedar Tree Neck, and Menemsha, together with a score of barrels of bottled Canadian ale, all evidently from the rum-runner *John Dwight* that had rolled over and sank off Cuttyhunk the day before. Seven of the bodies were wrapped in life preservers, and an eighth was found face down in a small boat, with the back of his skull crushed. Several days later, a large lifeboat was found at Quick's Hole with two holes stove in its sides, suggesting some survivors may have escaped the wreck. Over the next few days, strangers arrived on the Island at odd hours to view or claim the bodies. Several witnesses stated that one body was perfectly intact when it left Leland Renear's undertaking parlor in Vineyard Haven, but after it arrived in Cambridge at the direction of his purported brother, the body was found to have had its hands burned to prevent fingerprinting, and its eyes burned out. It was soon found that some of the other victims had died violent deaths, and had not drowned. Although the event was never fully explained, most islanders concluded that the *John Dwight* suffered not from an accident but rather from a massacre and robbery from competing rum-runners.

While the *John Dwight* incident was memorably tragic, rumrunning made regular Island news over the next decade. One stormy January morning in 1924, for instance, ninety cases of whiskey, together with a number of full kegs and barrels, were discovered ashore at Stonewall Beach on Chilmark's south shore, as was a large abandoned motorboat. Three men were seen making a getaway across the hills of Chilmark. The police suspected the nameless craft—possibly the *Caroline* of New Bedford—was a tender for a rumrunner, gone astray and grounded in the storm. The three men escaped, and the liquor was taken to the Coast Guard station at Gay Head.

THE HYDROPLANE

In July 1919, this Curtiss NC-3 hydroplane landed with great fanfare in Oak Bluffs after a bumpy two-and-a-half-hour flight from New York. Aboard were Melvin Fuller and Myron Brown, New York businessmen and East Chop summer residents, and their pilot, C. D. Griffin. This was not the very first flight to the Vineyard. That happened ten days earlier, when two seaplanes from the Naval Air Base in Chatham landed near the jetties in Oak Bluffs for a ninety-minute stop, but it made a huge sensation. The trio docked for the night at the Wesley House pier, where they were greeted with a celebratory supper at the hotel. Paying ten dollars apiece, adventurous souls lined up the

next morning to ride two at a time in the open cockpit, some with wads of cotton in their ears, a thousand feet in the air at a breathtaking sixty miles per hour. Seventy-four people flew that day, including a visiting young playwright, Eugene O'Neill. "Week-end commuting by airplane received an impetus," concluded the New York–based trade magazine, *Aerial Age Weekly*.

1919: *The False Faces*, a film starring Henry Walthall and Lon Chaney, was released. The hero, known only as "Lone Wolf," discovers the location of a secret German submarine base on the south shore of Martha's Vineyard after being picked up by a U-boat at sea. In the book on which the movie is based, author Louis Joseph Vance describes it as a "breach in the south coast line which permitted the utilisation of what had formerly been an extensive fresh-water pond as this secret submarine base." As a drunken Prussian sailor admitted to the Lone Wolf, "The sea made the breach during a gale, our people helped . . . Now we can enter a secluded, land-locked harbour with just enough water at low tide, and lie hidden there till the word comes to move again . . . and friends in plenty on the island to keep all our needs supplies—petroleum, fresh vegetables, champagne, all that . . ." The Vineyard appeared regularly in Vance's popular novels, including such works as *No Man's Land: A Romance*.

FRED METELL

An unidentified (but quite dapper) couple pose in front of their automobile on Circuit Avenue about 1920. Fred Metell, whose sign appears in the background, was a popular Oak Bluffs plumber who later sold the Island's first electric refrigerators. His father, José Pimental, arrived on the Vineyard in the 1870s from Flores Island in the

Azores; his name was corrupted to "Joseph P. Metell," and he became the progenitor of the Island's Metell family. The sign beyond reads "The Monohanset—Furnished Rooms," a hotel or boarding house presumably named after the Island's storied nineteenth-century steamer of the same name. The building on the left was the post office.

BATHERS

Three unidentified beachgoers show off their outfits at the "bathing beach" in Oak Bluffs about 1920. Bathers arrived fully clothed and then changed into their bathing costumes in one of the dozens of bathhouses visible on the left. Daredevils would dive from the wharves and rafts while others would climb the enormous boulder known as "Lover's Rock" (off-camera to the viewer's right), but most would forgo the water altogether or simply bathe. The steamer wharf is seen in the

distance where visitors would arrive on one of the aging sidewheel steamers that came from New Bedford and Woods Hole. Bathing was not a popular activity until the end of the nineteenth century, and until 1896 the Martha's Vineyard Railroad, connecting the steamer wharf to Katama's Mattakeesett Lodge, dominated much of this waterfront.

THE IMMIGRANTS

Martha's Vineyard has long been an island of immigrants. In 1905, more than a quarter of the residents of Oak Bluffs were foreign-born—mostly Portuguese-speaking immigrants from the Azores and

Cape Verde. By 1920, almost one-third of the Island's population were first- or second-generation immigrants. (By comparison, less than 10 percent of the Vineyard's modern population was born outside of the United States.)

"The Portuguese from the Azores are overrunning the Island" read one national 1894 newspaper story. "They will eventually form nine-tenths of the inhabitants. They are frugal and thrifty, and, as my driver expressed it, 'live on potatoes and turnips.'"

THE ARTIFICIAL POND

Oak Bluffs' parks are as old as the town itself. Designed in the late 1860s and early 1870s by landscape architect Robert Morris Copeland, the *Boston Globe* described them this way in 1875: "The parks are five in number, namely, Ocean Park, diamond shape; Niantic Park, triangular in form; Waban Park, a parallelogram; Pettuluma Park, a semi-circle; and Hartford Park, which contains a shady grove. These parks are magnificently laid out, and of course are among the attractions of the Vineyard. The trotting park [on the far end of Circuit Avenue] is a half-mile track, less than a mile from the steamboat wharf, and affords much pleasure to those who have brought fast horses to the sea-side." (Pettuluma Park was renamed Viera Park in 1968, and Waban was renamed Dennis Alley Park in the early 2000s.)

An 1880 map of Cottage City shows nine named and three unnamed parks in Oak Bluffs east of Circuit, together with another nine parks within the Campgrounds, plus a whopping twenty-four parks across the waters in Vineyard Highlands. (Alas, most of these are now residential home lots.)

But Ocean Park was the jewel of Oak Bluffs, the axis around which much of the early town was designed. By 1880 it was home to the fireworks and foot races of the annual Grand Illumination, and by 1885 it was crowned with a popular bandstand, where concerts were given every night in the summer. "One does not easily tire of the breezy freshness of Ocean Park," wrote the *New York Herald*.

Ocean Park, Oak Bluffs, Mass.

Pre-1930 postcard view labeled "The Lake, Ocean Park, Oak Bluffs"

The parks were almost lost to development. While designated as public spaces by the Oak Bluffs Land Company, the company never fully relinquished its legal claims to the land. So when the deeds were purchased by Boston speculator George Abbott in 1885, he demanded an outrageous sum of forty thousand dollars for Ocean Park alone, or he would "cut it up and build upon it." Residents and local authorities were "somewhat depressed," wrote the *Lowell Daily Courier*. But a battle was fought all the way to the Massachusetts Supreme Court, and in a decision by Oliver Wendell Holmes (later the legendary US Supreme Court justice), Oak Bluffs' parks were ruled to be forever open to the public.

A flurry of beautification followed. In 1893, the *Boston Globe* noted, "The improvements which have gradually been going on around this sea-girt isle for two or three years are commencing to tell, and the summer residents are rewarded for the money which they have so spent. Especially is this noticeable by the wonderful transformation made in Ocean Park. Three years ago this was nothing but a waste of seagrass

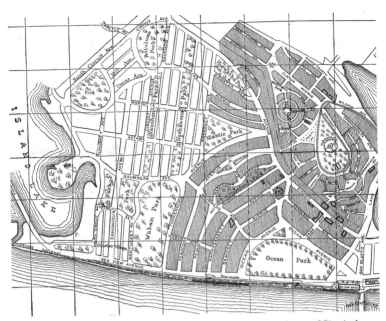

Detail from the 1880 Reid map of Cottage City showing one dozen parks east of Circuit Avenue

and sand. Now it is a smooth-shaved lawn, intersected with concrete walks, having a picturesque artificial pond in the center, which is bordered with tastefully arranged flower beds."

The "picturesque artificial pond" has changed shape and style over the years—most recently in 2001—but it has always been an important fixture of Ocean Park. Known as "the Children's Pool," "the Wading Pool," "the Boat Pool," or "the Lake," this concrete landmark has been used for 124 years to sail toy boats, and—for the fearless, anyway—to wade.

In a Facebook conversation about the pool, Bert Owens of Mashpee remembered, "I used to play in that pool as a tot in the mid-'40s. I used to sail little boats in there. A lot of children did. Not much actual wading; there were leeches in there. Creepy water—it was not aerated or kept clean. We stayed at the edges. I will not forget the leeches." Donna Honig of Edgartown adds, "In the '50s we always sailed small boats in it. Most of the time there was water in just one-half of it. My grandmother would not let us wade in it. Everyone was afraid of getting polio." But it didn't stop Bonnie Ciancio Parent of Edgartown—she writes, "I played in that park my whole childhood, as I grew up on Kennebec Avenue. We had small wooden boats with outboard motors on them. We waded in if it didn't make it to the other side. Lots of the Oak Bluffs neighborhood kids played in that park."

Alan Muckerheide of Oak Bluffs adds, "We rode our bicycles around that sloped edge and across the little connector/bridge in the late '60s to early '70s. Also on occasion, we rode through the middle, hoping to make it to the other side without falling in."

HARDING'S

W. D. Harding's clothing and shoe store stood on Circuit Avenue roughly where Reliable Market is today. Mr. Harding, a Vineyard Haven native who opened his shoe business as a young man in the 1870s, sold dry goods, clothing, and Queen Quality Shoes here until his death in 1917. Afterward, Mr. Harding's daughter Mary and her new husband, Clayton Hoyle, took over the business. Mr. Hoyle, a well-

Harding's Store, 1920. From left—Eva Phillips, Lucy Thomas, Mary Harding Hoyle, and Clayton Hoyle.

Clayton Hoyle poses with one of his celebrated fishing poles.

to-do Connecticut native remembered for his smart outfits and strong opinions, added a line of toys and children's items (including toy boats and firecrackers) to their stock.

But Hoyle was more interested in fishing than he was in women's shoes and toys. One of the founding members of the Rod and Gun Club, Hoyle was one of the fishermen credited with organizing the 1946 tournament that would later become the Martha's Vineyard Striped Bass and Bluefish Derby. (The Rod and Gun Club, located originally above Hoyle's store, is also remembered for the lively gambling sessions held there.)

Hoyle's homemade wood-and-leather fishing poles became a much-sought-after item among Vineyard fishermen. He is credited by many as the inventor of the first surfcasting reel, designed for fishermen to efficiently haul big fish in to shore. Soon after Hoyle's rod became a local hit, a large New York firm released a very similar rod that became nationally popular. Hoyle was never credited.

After Mrs. Hoyle's death in 1952, Mr. Hoyle closed the store, and opened an Oak Bluffs tackle shop, where he built and repaired rods and reels and sold his popular surfcaster.

THE TEA HOUSE

The Betty Benz Tea House served lunch and afternoon tea at the Lagoon Bridge until its destruction by hurricane. "For 'Tea' we serve a 'Betty Benz Special,' consisting of cinnamon toast, assorted sandwiches, hot or iced drinks, and homemade cake. Ice cream, too, if you want it," its owner exclaimed in a 1922 *Woman's Home Companion* feature.

While part of the building may once have served as the draw-tender's office, by 1915 it was already known as "the Tea House at the Bridge,"

The Betty Benz Tea House on the Vineyard Haven–Oak Bluffs bridge

or the Eagleston Tea House. It stood at street level on the approach to the original, hand-cranked drawbridge, which was much lower than subsequent drawbridges and crossed by the electric streetcars. A *New York Herald* columnist described "great earthen hanging baskets of brilliant geraniums, which brighten the pergola." The tea house was originally operated by dry goods merchant Allan P. Eagleston, who also founded the Eagle Theatre on Circuit Avenue (better known today as the "Island"). Eagleston and his brother opened a series of grand but short-lived dry goods stores in Vineyard Haven—the Vineyard Haven Cheap Store, the Boston Store, and the New York Store—as well a second movie theater, the Capawock.

By 1920 this shop had become the Hawaiian Tea House run by Hawaiian native and New York restaurateur Mary Wilder Gunn, featuring a full Hawaiian menu and decor, and by 1922 it became the Betty Benz Tea House, a prizewinner in the *Woman's Home Companion*'s "T-Room Contest," specializing in lobster and chicken dinners.

The Tea House after the 1944 hurricane

A landmark for decades, it was completely destroyed in the September 1944 hurricane. A private home was later built on this site, but demolished in 2013 to make room for a drawbridge.

1922: "Hinckley and Renear are planning extensive improvements to their building ... From this place they will conduct their undertaking business. All equipment will be modern with a large show-room in the front of the building which may be changed in a instant to a Chapel for conducting funeral services. In the rear of the building, it is said, will be the rooms of the Tisbury Chemical Company No. 1. The White Chemical will be kept here in a heated garage, the engine always warm and ready for business.... The department, although organized, is of the volunteer type and an alarm is necessary to call them together.... There must [always] be someone on hand who understands the intricacies of the White Chemical." [*Vineyard Gazette*]

STUDLEY'S

Clem Studley came to the Island as a toddler with his Yarmouth-born parents, and after a brief period selling tea in Providence with his brother, he and his wife Martha opened a grocery about 1910 in Oak Bluffs on the upper end of Circuit Avenue. By 1930 it had evolved into a hardware store.

Described as both "grave" and "dignified" but also as "the kindest of men," Studley was also credited for his good sense of humor. Martha, known less for humor and more for her nickname as "Queen of the

Studley's Grocery, Circuit Avenue, circa 1920s. Clem Studley is likely the gentleman on the far right.

Island," was described as "Victorian." Their daughter Barbara (known as "Bobby"), a member of the Oak Bluffs High School class of 1933, earned an English degree and moved to upstate New York and became a teacher.

Barbara's daughter Pat, a New York physician, writes, "I still have some things from the store. I have a wonderful floral painted tray, large, with the price tag still attached to it. I use it nearly daily during the summer. I have bean pots that I still use, and a pencil from the store."

1922: The Dukes County Teachers' Conference was held in Vineyard Haven, and Payson Smith, the Massachusetts state commissioner on education, was invited to the Island to speak. "Boys and girls of to-day are just as good and clean minded as the boys and girls of yesterday," the United News Service reported Payson declaring, in an article titled "Fears Elderly Flappers." "I am not disturbed at the danger cry of 'flappers.' The only flappers who worry me are the elderly ones who are aping the younger. They are the real menace."

JUMP SPARK JIM

James "Jump Spark Jim" West (1859–1948) presided over a Vineyard Haven antiques shop known as "The Shop of Unusual Things." His specialty was Vineyard whaling relics—captains' chests, lances he claimed Captain Cleveland carried on an 1847 voyage of the *Charles Morgan*, and the quarterboard of the *Ocmulgee*, among other treasures. His father, Benjamin West, was a lifelong Vineyard whaler who had sailed on the whaling ships *Java*, *Virginia*, and *Moctezuma*, and served as first mate of the *Chase*.

But the most unusual thing in the Shop of Unusual Things was undoubtedly West himself. He held an impressive range of occupations during his lifetime: gold prospector, Port Hunter salvager, jeweler, boat dealer, dredging engineer, cabinetmaker, fisherman, furniture dealer, fine artist, mattress dealer, upholsterer, and lastly, antiques dealer. He was known for his folksy (if sometimes bizarre) epigrams—"Jump Spark Jim Sayings"—which he published with every advertisement for his shop.

And the most prolific trade at his shop was certainly West's colorful autobiographical tales . . . like the time he dynamited a glacier in the Klondike during the gold rush and uncovered the frozen carcass of a mammoth, which he cooked and feasted on with his dogs. ("Good eating" he later told a *Boston Globe* reporter.) Or the time while working for the shipping firm of Holmes, Luce & Co. in Boston when he trapped fifty rats, anesthetized them with ether, hung little sleigh bells

"Jump Spark Jim" West at the Shop of Unusual Things

West's "Shop of Unusual Things" at Five Corners, c. 1926, now occupied by "Wicked Martha's"

on them, and turned them loose to jingle in the walls. A year later, one of his belled rats was caught in London and its picture published in *Strand* magazine, which West proudly displayed in his shop.

The *Ocmulgee* was one of a small handful of whaling ships, including the *Pocahontas*, *Malta*, and *Helen Augusta*, which was based out of Holmes Hole. (Edgartown had a few more; most Vineyard whalers worked out of New Bedford.) The *Ocmulgee* sailed on at least five successful whaling voyages to the Atlantic, Pacific, and Indian Oceans, and in 1849 became one of the very first whaling ships to pass through the Bering Strait and enter the Arctic Ocean to hunt bowheads. In 1862 the ship was captured and burned off the Azores as the first northern whaler sunk by the Confederate warship *Alabama* during the Civil War. Its quarterboard survived and eventually returned to the Vineyard—in 1908 it could be found hung over a boathouse door on South Water Street in Edgartown—and later ending up in West's shop. (Do any readers know its whereabouts today?)

OLD ISLAND COOKING

Want to prepare an authentically old-fashioned Vineyard meal for the holidays? Look no further than the *Island Cook Book*, published in 1924 as a fundraiser to build the new Martha's Vineyard Hospital. Favorite recipes were submitted from cooks across the Island, and money was raised from advertising and sponsorships by everyone from Brickman's to the Crowell Coal Company. The paperback was published by the Herald Printing Co. of Circuit Avenue.

From Lucinda Vincent's Prune Whip and Walnut Sandwiches to an Edgartown recipe for Banana Salad, it's all here. Four different recipes for brown bread, James Look's clam shortcake, salmon loaf, Helen Mayhew Anderson's English Potted Meat, mustard pickles, five recipes for doughnuts, and an Oak Bluffs recipe for mincemeat ("Cook slowly about all day"). Almah Jernegan's poultry dressing ("Put heart and gizzard in the pan. Let it get to cooking good . . .") comes with a disclaimer: "It may not sound appetizing, but please try it and you will change your mind."

Fresh fruits and vegetables are few and far between. The slim chapter titled "Vegetables" consists primarily of boiled recipes heavy with cream, eggs, or, in the case of Joseph Allen's Necessity Mess, a half-pound of "mixed pork."

A special section titled "For the Invalid" offers recipes used by Martha's Vineyard Hospital nurses. ("[We] will, we hope, answer the often-asked question 'What can I give my patient to eat?'") The chapter features such delicacies as Toast Water (pretty much what it sounds like, only finely strained), and Jelly and Ice (exactly what it sounds like).

In the "Sandwiches" chapter, an unidentified Edgartown cook offers a simple one: "Peanut butter made into a paste with marshmallow mist makes a dainty sandwich to go with the hearty ones."

For dessert, try some Molasses Sponge Cookies ("Delicious if made just right") or Clara Athearn's Fruit Cake ("Bake a long time") or Mrs. Norton's "Old Time 'Tilton Cake.'" (Be sure to substitute pork fat for the butter.)

Fundraising efforts were a success. Founded in 1921, the Martha's Vineyard Hospital opened its brand-new facility at its current location in 1929.

THE AUGUSTA

O n August 26, 1924, a hurricane swept the coast of New England. Crops were ruined, trees uprooted, highways flooded, and shipping virtually stopped along the Eastern Seaboard.

In heavy rain and fierce northeast winds, the freighter *Augusta*, an intercoastal shipping steamer that normally plied the waters between Boston and New York, was beached at Eastville. The crew remained aboard, as high seas prevented their escape, but they managed to stay out of danger.

Not far away, on the rocks off Cuttyhunk, the whaling bark *Wanderer*—the last of New Bedford's square-riggers—was wrecked on what was to have been its final voyage to the South Atlantic whaling grounds. Its crew abandoned ship in two open whaleboats. One boat was rescued by the Coast Guard and brought to Cuttyhunk; the other sheltered for the night on the lightship at Sow and Pigs Reef and came ashore the next day.

Meanwhile, off Nantucket Shoals, a one-hundred-foot wave swept over the White Star liner *Arabic*, injuring seventy-five transatlantic passengers, mostly immigrants, headed from Hamburg to New York City.

In Oak Bluffs, Siloam Avenue summer residents Dr. W. Louis Chapman, a Providence physician, and his wife Geneva were feared lost in the storm, as their small yacht had left the Vineyard just before the

The freighter Augusta, *stuck fast in the sand at Eastville after the unnamed hurricane of 1924*

hurricane hit, and they were not heard from for days afterward. (Fortunately, they later turned up intact.)

A horse in Vineyard Haven was electrocuted after stepping on a fallen wire, and in East Chop, roofs and porches were blown off. In Eastville, not far from where the *Augusta* beached, a summer bungalow was toppled from its foundations.

The day after the storm, the Coast Guard's revenue cutter *Acushnet* arrived to help pull the Augusta off the beach. By the end of the week, with the help of a wrecking lighter and heavy beach gear, the *Acushnet* managed to pull the grounded steamer's bow twenty feet off shore. The minimally damaged vessel was eventually freed.

1926: With one automobile to every 2.7 people, the town of West Tisbury claimed to hold the record for the largest per capita ownership of automobiles. The Island as a whole was home to 1,251 cars in total, including 639 Fords, 234 Buicks, seventy-five Dodges, and sixty-four Chevrolets.

THE ARTIST MYSTIC

Hanging in the staff room of the Edgartown Library is a ten-by-sixteen-inch oil painting titled *Scene at Cuttyhunk* signed by the artist, Frederic Thompson. Painted about 1908, this innocuous landscape belies a colorful Chilmark artist with a curious and convoluted story involving ghosts, poisonings, secret codes, hidden chambers, and the Mafia.

A New Bedford native, Frederic Louis Thompson attended the Swain School of Design (later integrated into UMass Dartmouth), and from the age of fourteen worked as a trophy designer, engraver, and modeler in both silver and gold. He married glass decorator Caroline Leonard of Cleveland, and they soon moved to New York City, where he found work designing for Tiffany & Co. and other jewelers before opening his own short-lived jewelry and engraving business. But shortly after the turn of the century, Thompson sold his business, quit work, and began full-time oil painting.

Thompson declared he had become possessed by the spirit of famous landscape painter (and Nonamesset Island native) Robert Swain Gifford, who had recently died in 1905. His formal art education conveniently forgotten, Thompson was portrayed by the press as an untalented tradesman who became suddenly and supernaturally endowed with Gifford's artistic gifts. He devoted all his time to landscape painting in Gifford's style, claimed of hearing the voice of the dead artist in his mind, and of dreaming and hallucinating windswept landscapes on the Elizabeth Islands and the Vineyard where Gifford had visited during his lifetime. He sketched to violin melodies no one else could hear, and said he sometimes felt as if he himself was Gifford. He became the subject of a full chapter in the popular 1919 supernatural text *Contact with the Other World*, written by Columbia University professor James Hyslop, who personally examined Thompson's behavior in great detail.

Thompson became an artistic success, making a lucrative living selling "spook pictures" in a number of prominent galleries around New York City, even selling one painting to author Mark Twain. The Thompsons began summering in Cuttyhunk. In 1908 they closely befriended a wealthy socialite twenty-five years their elder, Colonel Horace Brookes. ("Colonel" was an honorary rather than a military title, but that didn't stop Brookes from commissioning an oil portrait from Thompson in which he posed in an elaborate, gold-laced colonel's uniform.)

The Thompsons and Colonel Brookes began summering together in Menemsha in 1911, first at the boarding house known as the Homestead, and soon in a small summer cottage Thompson built nearby for the three of them. In 1917 Brookes bought a lot of land on South Road bordering Chilmark Pond, where they moved their home and expanded it to include a large fieldstone fireplace, carefully built by Thompson. They named the house "Crow's Pocket Camp," and the three lived together there every summer until 1925. Thompson soon gave up painting altogether, instead spending all day measuring lobsters, fish, crabs, and leaves for an obsessive new theory he was developing on the "proportional growth of life" that he felt "coordinated" with Einstein's theories and could be applied to automobile and airplane design.

In 1925, the Thompsons' marriage fell apart. Caroline would later allege that he choked her, hit her, tried to force pills on her, tried to smash her head with a rock, and threatened to kill her on a number of occasions. He moved abruptly to Florida that fall. He claimed afterward that he had received a letter with a West Tisbury postmark signed by the "Black Hand"—reputedly an appendage of the Mafia—threatening to kill Caroline if he didn't leave for Miami immediately and cease all contact with her. Caroline quickly divorced him in his absence, on grounds of cruelty. When Thompson learned of the divorce, he filed a half-million dollar lawsuit against Colonel Brookes for "alienation of affection," claiming the eighty-three-year-old man's affair with his wife had ended their marriage.

Then Caroline discovered a loose stone in the Crow's Pocket fireplace revealing a large hidden chamber. Inside she found incriminating letters to Thompson's alleged mistresses, some in "hieroglyphic" code, together with "obscene literature" and other odd items. More letters soon came to light, suggesting that Thompson had attempted to poison his wife with arsenic-laced fruit on a number of occasions in 1925, and that he had attempted to mail her a box of poisoned candy during his absence in Florida.

Thompson was arrested in November 1929 in New York, extradited, and locked in the Edgartown jail to face two charges of attempted murder. He was confined to the Massachusetts Hospital for the Criminally Insane at Bridgewater for observation, remaining there for fifty-two days. The trial of the "psychical artist" in Edgartown the following spring was followed by newspapers in Boston, New York, and beyond. In his defense, Thompson claimed that Caroline had forged all of the incriminating letters, and produced a handwriting expert to testify on his behalf. After three days of heated testimony and three-and-a-half hours of deliberation at the Edgartown courthouse, Capt. Hartson Bodfish, foreman of the jury, announced the verdict: not guilty on both counts.

Thompson immediately sued Brookes and Caroline for one million dollars in damages. Caroline countersued for a million. The lawsuits dragged on for years in court, with little satisfaction on either side. Caroline and Brookes continued to live together in their South Road home until their deaths in 1935 and 1954, and the three were embroiled in suits, countersuits, and appeals for the rest of their long lives. In one of the last countersuits, Caroline sued Thompson for one million dollars on the grounds that he had "annoyed her to an unbearable degree."

Thousands of pages of colorful testimony and bizarre evidence from Thompson's trial in Edgartown and subsequent suits can be read for free in Google Books.

GEORGE SALVADORE

George Washington Salvadore of Edgartown was the world's third-ranking welterweight boxer. Described as "rugged" and a "hoofer" measuring less than five feet, nine inches, he was often referred to in the national press as "the Portuguese Welterweight." The youngest of eleven children of Azorean immigrant Antone Salvadore and his wife Mary, George was born and raised on the Great Plains of Edgartown at his parents' farm. But as the *Brooklyn Daily Eagle* wrote, "Ever since he was a kid in rompers, George could make his feet talk."

Salvadore got his chance at fame in the summer of 1928, when more than a thousand spectators showed up in Oak Bluffs to watch the first of a series of professional boxing matches on Martha's Vineyard, run by the Antler's Club at Dreamland Rink. Salvadore's first professional match ended in a knockout as he sent veteran boxer Johnny Mello of Fall River to the mat.

More than a few Vineyard boxers began professional prizefighting runs during this brief era, like welterweight Henry "Heck" Benefit of Edgartown (known as the "Katama Wildcat"), a group of tough Oak Bluffs boys named Billy "Young" Randolph, Jack Macey, Augustus Amaral, and Jimmy Jerome; and Bob Waller of Edgartown. But none came close to Salvadore's fame. He soon became a "name" fighter, featured on bills across the country and drawing thousands of fans.

Salvadore's career spanned 123 bouts, including forty-eight wins (nineteen KOs), thirty-five losses, and ten draws. As the Depression deepened and interest in hosting professional boxing on the Vineyard waned, he moved to Houston, and then to San Francisco. In 1936 he was taken under the management of Joe Gould, best known as manager of heavyweight champion Jim "Cinderella Man" Braddock, whom Salvadore traveled the country with. (Braddock and Gould were played by Russell Crowe and Paul Giamatti in the 2005 biopic *Cinderella Man*.)

On December 12, 1938, at National Hall in the Mission District of San Francisco, Salvadore was matched with the welterweight champion of China, Andre "The Hammer" Shelaeff, an undefeated eighteen-year-old Russian sensation who had arrived in the United States just four months earlier. Both men fought hard that night, neither were knocked down, and Salvadore ultimately won on a decision. Shelaeff returned unaided to his dressing room, but then collapsed. He died later that night at the hospital; cause of death: "brain concussion." Salvadore was charged with manslaughter, but was soon exonerated by a coroner's jury.

It was Salvadore's last fight. He hung up his gloves and never fought again.

GEORGE ALLEY'S EDGARTOWN MARKET

When we think of "Alley's store" today, there's only one that comes to mind—the old S. M. Mayhew Co. general store in West Tisbury, bought by Albion Alley at the end of World War II. But in the first half of the twentieth century, "Alley's" could have been any one of several stores down-Island run by Albion's older cousins, George and Antone Alley of Oak Bluffs.

George Alley (born George Pachico Medeiros) was the son of Cottage City grocer Domingo Pacheco Medeiros, an immigrant from the island of São Miguel in the Azores, and his German wife Lena Knoff. Marianne Thomas writes in her book *Our Portuguese Heritage*, "Family lore has it that the surname 'Alley,' a play on halibut, was derived from a nickname given to [Domingo's brother] Antone when, as a teenager in Cottage City, he peddled fish in the Portuguese community. Whatever its origins, the name was thought to be far easier to deal with than 'Medeiros,' and it was adopted by nearly all of the family members."

George and his brother Tony, growing up as clerks in their father's grocery, became known as the Alley Brothers. They opened the Public Market in downtown Vineyard Haven, which would later become Cronig's, and then opened the Alley Brothers Public Market in Montgomery Square, Oak Bluffs. George was the butcher, and later in life worked as the meat cutter at the First National Store in Edgartown.

George Alley's Edgartown Market, about 1929

A large flyer for a boxing match is visible on the far right. The boxing craze reached its height on Martha's Vineyard in 1929. Professional matches took place regularly at Dreamland Rink in Oak Bluffs during the warmer months.

DARLING'S

In addition to saltwater taffy and "Cottage City Pop Corn," Darling's also sold potato chips, peanuts, "log cabin rolls," fudge, mints, Vermont caramels, and maple candies in their very popular Oak Bluffs store. Its motto—"For Twenty Years the Best"—was in prominent use long after the twentieth anniversary of its circa 1900 opening (and, oddly, well before: 1907 or even earlier).

Owner Carroll J. Darling was a summertime Kennebec Avenue resident who hailed from the tiny village of Albany in northern Vermont, where his father ran Darling's Hotel. Each winter the Darlings would return to Vermont, where Carroll was the biggest stockholder in the Cary Maple Sugar Company, at one time the largest wholesale maple sugar company in North America. Cary Maple Sugar (today part of the Maple Grove Farms brand) was then used principally to flavor plug tobacco and cigarettes.

Darling's, Circuit Avenue, about 1929

Sara and Carroll John Darling

Darling's was a successful mainstay of Circuit Avenue for most of the twentieth century. In 1912, Darling exhibited his state-of-the-art motor-driven popcorn and candy machinery at the Boston Electrical Show, and in 1924 he purchased the nearby Eagle Theater at the bottom of Circuit Avenue. Upon his death in 1936, ownership of Darling's was passed to his nephew, Harris Carr.

A poster, visible at the far left of the photo on page 190, advertises Mal Hallett's orchestra at the Tivoli Ballroom. Hallett, a jazz violinist from Boston, was at the height of his career and known for such popular hits as 1926's "She's a Cornfed Indiana Girl (But She's Mama to Me)."

1929: Thieves used explosives to break into the safe of the Steamboat Company in a freight shed at the end of the Oak Bluffs wharf one night. The Labor Day weekend receipts, including those collected from four thousand passengers on Monday alone, amounted to fifteen thousand dollars. An estimated ten thousand dollars was stolen by the thieves. The *Boston Globe* called it "the largest robbery the county has ever known."

Fortunately, steamship clerk H. W. Rowe had marked a five-dollar bill given to him by a female friend the night before, as a romantic memento. He planned to replace it the next day. The marked bill turned up a month later, and became the first clue in solving the case. Joseph Fisher of Providence and Edward Tracy of Woonsocket were arrested, and Arthur Carpenter of Vineyard Haven was detained as a material witness. Tracy was found guilty and sentenced to fifteen to eighteen years in state prison.

PART VI
LATER TALES

ZEPPELIN OVER
GAY HEAD

An airship floats past the Gay Head Cliffs in the late 1920s or early 1930s, to the delight of chilly onlookers.

Dan Grossman of Airships.net identifies this vessel as the US Navy's ZR-3, the USS *Los Angeles*. Built in Germany by the Zeppelin Company, the ZR-3 was delivered to the US Navy in 1924 in what was to be the world's last nonstop transatlantic flight until Lindbergh's famous solo flight in 1927. It was over 650 feet long, with a crew of forty-three, and built with all the accommodations of a long-distance commercial

airliner, including sleeping compartments and a first-class galley. For the next eight years, this helium-filled airship flew hundreds of good-will, publicity, and training flights around the United States and as far south as the Panama Canal. Its final flight was in 1932.

The Gay Head Life Saving Station is visible in the photo at cliff's edge directly below the passing airship.

1930: The *Vineyard Gazette*'s cheeky "'Round 'Bout Tisbury" column reported: "Patrons of the Vineyard Store are viewing with astonishment the new stepladder standing behind the candy counter. The ladder contains but five steps, but the weight of the material is what causes surprise. Timber such as is used to frame stables and grain elevators is used for the framework, while the treads are of wharf planking. Mr. Tilton, proprietor, explains the ordinary type of stepladder will only support about a ton and Big Hutch has stepped through so many that the overhead has increased noticeably; hence the specially constructed piece of furniture. The ladder was constructed at the shop of William E. Dugan and brought to the store by building movers, according to report." Kenneth "Big Hutch" Hutchinson presided over the soda fountain beside his brother, "Little Hutch," for decades at Tilton's (later Yates's) drugstore in Vineyard Haven.

THE BOSTON HOUSE

Krikor Barmakian was born in 1883 in Malatya—a large city in what is now central Turkey, a hundred miles from the Syrian border—in what was then a part of the Ottoman Empire known as Western Armenia. Amid the great massacres of ethnic Armenians that would soon lead to the Armenian Genocide, Krikor immigrated to the United States in the early 1900s with his wife Yester (Esther) and was soon joined by his siblings and mother. Departing from the family trade of jewelry-making, Krikor opened a series of restaurants—in Cleveland, Somerville, and then Providence.

In the early 1920s while on a recreational day trip to Oak Bluffs, Krikor spotted an empty storefront for rent. He was "rather impulsive," remembers his nephew Vaughn Barmakian, and "a little bit of a maverick," invariably adorned with a three-piece suit, pocket watch, diamond ring, and cigar. Acting on a whim, Krikor leased the summer boarding house and dining room known originally as the Cottage City House (built in the 1870s or early 1880s). He converted it first into a successful ice cream parlor, then into a cafe and hotel: The Boston House.

Throughout the 1920s, the Boston House was advertised as an "American and Chinese Restaurant and Cafeteria" featuring homemade pastry. ("He always had a Chinese chef to cook both ways," recalls Vaughn.) He also advertised "attractive rooms at reasonable prices,"

Krikor "Jerry" Barmakian poses with an El Producto cigar outside the original Boston House on Circuit Avenue, where Ryan Amusements is today.

although these quickly filled with Krikor's siblings and their families for the summer.

Late one night in December 1938, a fire broke out in H. L. Butler's tailor shop in nearby Haines Block. An alley cat alerted Esther to the fire, and she was the first to call the alarm. The Barmakians escaped with only their bedclothes. Despite the efforts of dozens of firemen, the Boston House and the Haines Block were both completely destroyed, together with the Japanese gift store between them. Other buildings, including the Island House and Darling's candy shop, also suffered serious damage. Losses were estimated as high as a quarter of a million dollars. Fortunately, no one was injured.

With the help of his poker buddies (DeSorcy, Hinckley, and Sweet at the Rod and Gun Club over Hoyle's Department Store), Krikor soon borrowed enough money to rebuild the Boston House, a building that still stands today on Circuit Avenue. When the Second World War broke out, Barmakian found that he held the only year-round liquor license on the Island. Each night buses full of thirsty servicemen from the naval air station would arrive looking for beer and whiskey. Barmakian repaid his debts in two years, mostly through the sale of wartime beer: an eight-ounce glass for ten cents, or a bottle for a quarter. Young Vaughn and his twin brother Diran were tasked with fetching ice from the basement. It was "raucous," he recalls; "It was an exciting way to grow up." So much beer was sold so quickly, he remembers, that once a keg was spiked open, "they never shut the tap." Many of these servicemen, he later learned, were killed at Normandy on D-Day.

After a bad stroke in 1946 rendered Krikor paralyzed on one side, the business was sold to George Munro (1915–1995). It became "Munro's Boston House," and while it became more of a respectable restaurant than a raucous tavern, it remained a Circuit Avenue landmark into the early 1980s.

1931: Frank Wood, respected superintendent of the Edgartown Water Company during the 1920s, was arrested for bungling a "stick-up" of the Holliston Savings Bank with a teenage partner. After a long career in banking, Wood came to the Island with his family to take a job as a grocery clerk for the S. M. Mayhew Company in West Tisbury, and then as the manager of their branch store in Chilmark as well as assistant Chilmark postmaster, before starting with the water company. After several years, he was dismissed by the company for "irregularities"—none criminal—and left the island. He tried to interest a female Boston doctor to back him in a "freak museum" venture, but when that fell through, he took to bank robbery.

OWEN PARK, 1932

Vineyard Haven natives Ralph Look (1910–1985) and Stan Lair (1902–1987) reminisced about early-twentieth-century winters in a series of recorded interviews:

Mr. Look: "Oh, sure. I've skated from East Chop to West Chop, back when I was eight or nine years old. Cold! You don't see that today . . . I've seen it 32 below zero, too! The day that Henry Cronig's house burned down at West Chop, it was 32 degrees below zero, might have been for two or three hours. On this Island, that's the truth!"

Owen Park and Vineyard Haven Harbor, about 1932. The Bethel's *launch* Helen May *is the large vessel visible on the right; the little black dots on the left are people, venturing dangerously out onto the ice.*

Mr. Lair recalled a favorite sledding hill, near the south side of Owen Park, known as Doane's Hill:

"Some of the more adventurous kids would start up on William Street, which meant sliding directly across Main Street, just hoping no cars would be going by. I guess they were lucky, 'cause I don't recall any accidents there. And then slide on down the hill to the harbor, right onto the harbor ice. Less traffic in those days."

Mr. Look: "I've gone down Doane's Hill there, sliding, see? Right out to the breakwater, see? That's a steep hill . . . I remember an incident of Herb Tilton going down ahead of me, and the harbor was all frozen over. Somewhere or other he got off of the sled and he went right under the ice. Someone aboard [a boat] pulled him out of there. If he hadn't of, he wouldn't be here today. Right under."

DON'T DO THIS

Vineyard Haven Harbor freezes over occasionally, although saltwater ice can be deadly to venture out on. In the old days, even the steamers were sometimes iced in. Woods Hole would close for days at a time, and ferries, when they were able to get out, would have to push through the inlet known as Robinson's Hole, between Naushon Island and Pasque Island, to get to New Bedford. In the 1930s, Dr. Raymond Merchant, whose office and home were on Main Street, would sometimes walk out on the ice to make house calls to vessels in the harbor.

Historian Henry Franklin Norton wrote of the harsh winter of 1778 in his book *Martha's Vineyard.* It came at the end of what had already been a dreadful year for Islanders, considering that British redcoats had

1933. Don't do this.

plundered nearly all of the Island's livestock and provisions that fall in the infamous Grey's Raid. According to Norton, that bitter winter nearly finished them off. He wrote, "The snow in some places was up to the second-story windows, and the ice was so thick that it was possible to drive with horse and sleigh to New Bedford . . . In December, after a terrible northeast blizzard, a school of black bass was found frozen in Lagoon Pond. People from all parts of the Island hurried to the pond and cut tons of fish out of the ice for food, thereby saving many from starvation."

CANDY & TOOTHPASTE

Pearson's Drug Store was located in the part of the Arcade building occupied today by Sharky's Cantina on Circuit Avenue in Oak Bluffs. Druggist William H. Pearson (1870–1934) moved to Oak Bluffs with his family and his pharmacy business in the mid-1920s. His Oak Bluffs shop was perhaps best remembered for its soda fountain and his variety of tasty candies, but this early photo shows a few of his other products, including "Colgate's Dental Cream," "Colgate Refill Shaving Stick," "Russell's Chocolates," and cigars. Pearson had operated drugstores in Lowell and Dorchester since the 1890s, but his final, Vineyard venture lasted only for perhaps a decade before his death at the age of sixty-four.

His name and store lived on under a series of owners for decades after his death, selling medicines, film (and twenty-four-hour photo finishing service), sunglasses, beach toys, sandwiches, and lime rickeys into the 1970s.

Ms. Bert Owens, now of Mashpee, remembers:

> The Smith family operated it in the 50s. My best childhood friend was their only daughter. They lived in an apartment upstairs, and we spent many hours playing in the large front room. They had a wonderful wind-up Victrola there, in a tall cabinet. They had a piano in the living room, and we would play

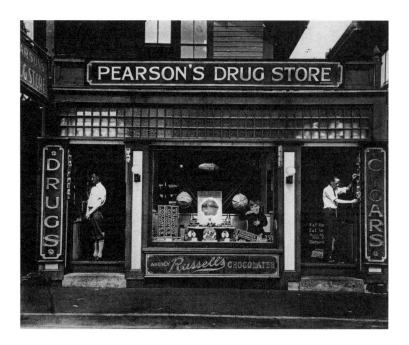

"Chopsticks." Mr. Smith had a great large radio in a cabinet, and we could hear radio from around the world, as I remember. He died around 1956, I believe.

There was the pharmacy, and then the wonderful soda fountain, a long marble slab. We were into the ice cream after closing, when we were cleaning up. We had a great time making sodas, milkshakes, frappes, and decadent ice cream sundaes. They kept hot butterscotch and hot chocolate going all the time open, plus marshmallow, fruit and nuts toppings all sorts of soda flavors. We loved the ice cream floats. The pharmacy kept busy, but the soda fountain was the draw.

By the late 1970s, the drugstore had been renamed "Arcade Drug Store."

1935: "More Than Third of Island Population is on Relief," reported the *Vineyard Gazette*, with 36 percent—some 1,820 Islanders—supported on public welfare. Oak Bluffs led with the highest figures in southeast Massachusetts, with more than 68 percent of its population on relief. In 1936, the Federal Commodity Distribution Center and warehouse moved from Oak Bluffs to Lane's Block in Vineyard Haven under the watch of county supervisor Capt. Chester Robinson, and in cooperation with the town welfare board.

AIR TALES

New York City holdup man Lewis "Bum Dogs" Miller was on the run in the spring of 1929 after committing a series of armed robberies with his partner, Landers "Pork Chops" Samuels, in Queens. Samuels was captured, but Miller fled to Oak Bluffs, where he took refuge in a bungalow. He couldn't hide long from the law, however. When Queens police detectives got word of Miller's whereabouts, they initially balked at the long drive and off-season ferry schedule; instead they decided to hire an airplane pilot to fly them to the Island. It was evidently the first time a plane had been used for this purpose, at least in this area, and their trip made the papers as far away as Indiana. Miller was soon captured and returned to Queens.

Seaplanes had been a regular sight on the Vineyard ever since the first "hydroplanes" arrived in Oak Bluffs in 1919. In 1926, two naval airmen fell to their deaths into Vineyard Haven Harbor after their seaplane nosedived and broke in two shortly after takeoff.

In 1932, aviator Charles Lindbergh used a seaplane to search the Vineyard's north shore for a yacht where he would purportedly find his kidnapped son, according to a ransom note. While the mysterious circling plane attracted much local attention, Lindbergh's search failed. (Twenty-month-old Charles Jr. would later be found dead near their New Jersey home.)

A seaplane ties up at Union Wharf. Regularly scheduled commercial flights provided service from both Edgartown and Vineyard Haven harbors to off-Island destinations during the 1930s.

By the early 1930s, a regularly scheduled commercial summer flight service was established with a twelve-passenger seaplane, connecting Vineyard Haven Harbor by air with New York and Nantucket. A pontoon leak in 1934 resulted in a delay in Vineyard Haven on one flight; the *Fitchburg Sentinel* reported, "It was the first time locally that an airship has been hauled out of the water in a ship's cradle to be repaired in a shipyard."

Regular seaplane service operated in Edgartown as well. In 1937 a Cape Cod Airlines flight full of New Yorkers crashed broadside into a laundry truck on the Chappy ferry while landing. Ferry captain Foster Silvia and truck driver Malcolm Keniston leaped from the moving ferry into the water to safety, but Charles Johnson of Edgartown suffered a serious head injury from the truck. The plane went down in twelve feet of water with all four passengers, but quick-thinking Coast Guardsmen on a nearby cutter came to their rescue. Miraculously, the air passengers were only shaken up, and none was seriously injured. Keniston is said to

Raul Medeiros of Vineyard Haven sits atop what is probably the 1944 wreckage of a Navy torpedo bomber that crashed north of the airport. [Photo courtesy Kathy Rogers.]

have kept a large piece of fabric from the fuselage rolled up in his attic until his death in 2004.

An elderly couple from New York making their first flight in 1940 weren't so lucky. Their seaplane hit a submerged object in Vineyard Haven Harbor upon landing, and overturned. The couple were killed. The pilot and a six-year-old passenger survived.

In 1944, a Navy pilot crash-landed a torpedo bomber in the scrub oak "two miles northeast of the Martha's Vineyard Naval Airport" following an engine fire, and overturned. While two enlisted men jumped clear, the pilot was trapped under the burning wreck. Two crash crews from the Naval Air Base soon arrived on the scene, and after an hour managed to extinguish the fire and free the trapped pilot. The three airmen suffered only cuts and bruises.

In 1947, two Barnstable men were charged with hunting wild Canadian geese from a seaplane in Edgartown. The hunters would allegedly shoot the geese from the air, and then land on the water to pick them up. State conservation officer J. Edward Bannister used a rented amphibious plane in his investigation, culminating on one occasion in an air chase in which the wily hunters outmaneuvered him and escaped. Nevertheless, the men were soon identified and charged.

1937: Police seized nine slot machines and made six arrests in Oak Bluffs on charges of setting up and promoting a lottery, after complaints by a number of residents. Those arrested included two proprietors of a bathing beach where one machine was located, a man at the bowling alley, two men employed at the Tivoli Taxi office where four machines were found, and the resident of a house on Oak Bluffs Avenue where three additional machines were found. Plainclothesmen had "spent considerable time securing evidence," noted the *Boston Globe*. Police had staged a similar raid two years earlier.

ORLIN DAVIS'S OXEN

Chilmark farmer Orlin Davis (1863–1947) stands atop an ox-pulled load of hay at his farm on Middle Road. Behind him is Philip Drew Jr. (1906–1983), and directing the yoke is Ernest Norton (1872–1945).

This photograph was probably taken in the late 1930s, when Drew and Norton lodged at the Davis home and Drew was employed as his

farm laborer. The Davis farm straddled the West Tisbury line, near Tiasquam River and close to what is now Brookside Farm. Davis was known for his Guernsey cows and won the occasional award on "Cattle Day" at the agricultural fair, but he is perhaps best remembered for the plane that crashed in his cow pasture during World War II.

1941: Three soldiers from the 101st Field Artillery Regiment at Camp Edwards, after a few drinks, wandered into Edgartown's volunteer fire station and found it deserted. So they took the forty-five-foot ladder truck out for a joy ride—the wrong way up a one-way street, past a local policeman standing in his yard, and past the state police barracks. Followed by a crowd of locals concerned there was a fire, the truck hit several parked cars and finally crashed into the Edgartown Library. [Boston Globe]

CAPTAIN IVORY

Captain John J. Ivory, artist, sits at his home, the permanently beached vessel *Dry Tortugas*, on Vineyard Haven Harbor, near the location of the present Black Dog Tavern.

The original inhabitant of this little boat was Canadian sailor Charles Hamilton, a long-term patient at the US Marine Hospital. Stan Lair (1902–1987) of Vineyard Haven recalled Mr. Hamilton: "He was very badly crippled. He was bent over, almost at a right angle from his waist, and he walked with two canes. He did quite a bit of work, though. He had a little shipyard. He built small boats down on the beach. At one time he lived in a boat—I guess a fire went out there in the stove or something; anyway, he froze to death, I believe, in that boat. And then later it was occupied by John Ivory, who did paintings, Grandma Moses–type paintings, mostly of ships, boats as he remembered them, and I guess they're quite valuable now."

Many colorful stories have been told about Captain Ivory—many by John Ivory himself—and it is difficult now to separate fact from fancy. Jane Slater of Over South Antiques in Chilmark is the last surviving member of the John Ivory Society, founded by Ted Hewitt, Stewart Bangs, and Bill Honey after Captain Ivory's death to identify and catalog Ivory's paintings. Of Captain Ivory's life, Ms. Slater says, "There's a lot of folklore."

Captain Ivory at home

What's fairly certain is that he spent his youth aboard clipper ships plying international waters, and spent time living in China and Japan. He settled in Oak Bluffs in the early 1900s, starting a family and working odd jobs as a mechanic and hotel cook before embarking on a second far-flung career as a merchant mariner. Returning to the Vineyard in the 1930s, he turned to painting, and to drink. A kindly man who welcomed visitors to his little vessel-home on the beach, his good nature was sometimes taken advantage of by tourists and collectors, who would buy his paintings for next to nothing. Some of his paintings show nail holes, it's remembered, from affixing his work to the underside of a table to deter burglars while he was away from his unlocked boat home. He painted on anything and everything—cardboard, linoleum, plywood, canvas, and scraps that people would bring him. He used house paint discarded by the neighboring lumberyard, and it's said he would sometimes make brushes from his own hair. He would sometimes draw on quahog shells and leave them on the beach for kids to find.

Ms. Slater donated the John Ivory Society's catalog and notes to the Vineyard Haven Public Library, together with a dozen of his paintings on long-term loan. One of the paintings still on display in the rear of the library is of the *Governor Robie*, a favorite subject he painted many times over. The *Governor Robie* was among the last of the merchant sailing ships in the China trade, and the one on which Ivory spent his boyhood under the command of Captain Nickels of Maine. In the corner of his painting he signed "1894 / Painting by a member of crew / Capt. J.J. Ivory / Master Mariner / Memmories."

1943: The wartime "dimout" was lifted in Vineyard Haven. "Shop and store windows were unshrouded for the first time in a year and a half," reported the *Vineyard Gazette*.

JACKLYN LAIR'S CARTOONS, 1947-1949

While cleaning out a closet, Jackie Baer of Vineyard Haven unearthed a trove of drawings she had secretly made on the back of old index cards during her years attending Tisbury High School in the late 1940s. Between 1947 and 1949 (her freshman, sophomore, and junior years), young Jacklyn Lair made hundreds of little cartoons depicting the real-life antics of her childhood friends, teachers, and a few other familiar Vineyard Haven folks. While the times have changed somewhat, teenagers were always teenagers. Here are a few of her drawings and the cast of characters who appeared in them.

"The time on the way to a fire a bunch of boys jumped on the car in town + embar-rassed us to death. September, 1948."

"Study Hall, Tisbury High School, 1948."

"When Janet ordered a pile of groceries and then told George to try and sell them. Freshman, 1947."

"The time we tried Neil's cigars. It was his birthday. August, 1948."

Cast of characters

Jacklyn Lair ("me")
Connie Frank
Franny Bettencourt
Janet Frieh
Ralph Packer
Neil Welch
Justin "Jud" Welch
George Conoyer (grocer)

1948: "Television is Here!" announced Phillips Hardware in an advertisement in the *Vineyard Gazette*. The sets were priced at $325 at their
Oak Bluffs store. But television has a much older connection to the Island:
Vineyard Haven summer resident Dr. Frank Jewett was proclaimed the
"inventor of television" by the *Gazette* in 1927. President of Bell Telephone
Laboratories, Dr. Jewett oversaw one of the first and most dramatic
demonstrations of the new medium earlier that year.

DAVE NOBLE, W1SGL

David Noble came to Martha's Vineyard in 1933 as a patient at the Marine Hospital in Vineyard Haven. Formerly employed on an oil tanker, Mr. Noble was slowly freezing up; he suffered from a creeping debility that ultimately left him almost completely paralyzed. By the time he turned forty, Noble was unable to leave the bed in the small home on Mount Aldworth that he shared with his sister Olive. Unable to walk, sit up, or even turn his head, he couldn't even read, because of eyestrain and his inability to hold a book or magazine. He only had full use of his right hand and his voice.

In 1949 Noble turned to ham radio. Friends set up a radio set and transmitter for him, cleverly adapted to accommodate his disabilities. He quickly earned his amateur radio license and call sign—W1SGL—and went on to become a familiar voice on the airwaves, speaking with "hams" from all over the earth, and tracking his conversations on the world map he hung on his wall. Vineyard hams would gather each week in his home in an informal club meeting, and Noble began to collect QSL cards—personalized postcards traditionally traded by hams after each new contact. This photograph became Noble's QSL card. His niece Kathie Noble Case of Edgartown, who moved to the Island with her family in her childhood to care for her uncle, writes, "He did radio right up until his death in '68. It was what we believed kept him alive all those years."

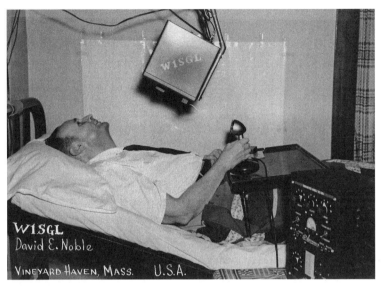

Dave Noble, W1SGL

1955: A six-foot, twelve-hundred-pound leatherback turtle, mortally wounded from a boat propeller, was discovered on an Edgartown beach in 1955. Police chief Fred Worden was called to put it out of its suffering with his pistol. "I've never handled anything exactly like this before," he concluded to a *Vineyard Gazette* reporter.

TONY THE SCISSOR MAN

Antonio "Tony the Scissor Man" DeCarlo walked the streets of Martha's Vineyard every summer, mending umbrellas, sharpening knives, and grinding scissors for local customers. Wielding a 150-year-old brass schoolbell once used by his father, he rang out his services in a three-beat waltz, calling out "Umbrellas to mend! Umbrellas to mend! Knives and scissors sharpened! Scissor grinder!" His forty-plus-pound backpack contained a massive Carborundum wheel in a wooden frame, which he drove by pumping a treadle with his foot.

DeCarlo hailed from Manhattan, the son and grandson of traveling "grinders" from the mountains of Campobasso province in southern Italy. By the 1960s, New York City's last seven pack-carrying grinders were all members of his extended family. It was a dying trade, even in Antonio's time, as home electric sharpeners competed with these lifelong professionals.

The Vineyard was far from DeCarlo's only territory—his summer route included Nantucket, Hyannis Port, Bar Harbor, and other New England coastal towns. He spent winters working the streets of St. Petersburg, Florida, and springtime on his native island of Manhattan, where he had plied his trade since 1904. He claimed to walk more than a dozen miles every day, six days a week. He worked until his death in 1967.

Inheriting his profession, route, and bell, his oldest son Dominick "Dom" DeCarlo brought sharpening services next to the Vineyard,

Tony DeCarlo, the traveling grinder, on his regular visit to the Vineyard.

together with his younger brother Fred. Dom boasted of walking thirty-one hundred miles a year and grinding over two hundred thousand knives and scissors annually. Heavyset, spectacled, and usually adorned by a Panama hat or baseball cap, Dom began using a modified golf cart to get his equipment around. His brother Fred used a truck.

Social networking has become an important historical research tool, in this case Facebook's "I Grew Up on Martha's Vineyard" group. A post of this photo, initially identified only as "Mr. DeCarlo," quickly brought a flood of information. DeCarlo's vocation as an itinerant "grinder" was identified in less than ten minutes and another twenty or so people quickly weighed in with their memories of Mr. DeCarlo working the streets of Skiff Avenue, Tuckernuck Avenue, Franklin Street, West Chop, State Road, Edgartown, and elsewhere.

Patricia Campos Manzoni writes, "The 'umbrella man' used to walk in the neighborhoods ringing his bell. He also sharpened knives, but we always called him the 'umbrella man.' He was around in the '50s."

Judith Leonard Culver writes, "Every summer the scissors man would stroll down our back street and sharpen all the scissors Mum had. I believe he did hedge trimmers also. His bell was a sure sign of summer."

Michael Anthony writes, "I remember him stopping in front of our house and we stood in the front yard while Mom brought out the knives and scissors to be sharpened. Everything happened on Skiff Avenue!"

While Tony is just a fond memory now, his eighty-one-year-old son Fred DeCarlo and grandson Darren DeCarlo are still following the family trade in their "KnifeMobile" in New York City, sometimes driving into the Hamptons on weekends, and still serving Floridians each winter, but no longer, alas, visiting Martha's Vineyard.

INDEX